Why the Amish Sing

YOUNG CENTER BOOKS IN ANABAPTIST & PIETIST STUDIES

Donald B. Kraybill, *Series Editor*

Why the Amish Sing

Songs of Solidarity & Identity

D. Rose Elder

Foreword by Terry E. Miller

JOHNS HOPKINS UNIVERSITY PRESS
Baltimore

This book was brought to publication with the generous assistance of the Lloyd Hibberd Endowment of the American Musicological Society, funded in part by the National Endowment for the Humanities and the Andrew W. Mellon Foundation.

Johns Hopkins University Press
2715 North Charles Street
Baltimore, Maryland 21218-4363
www.press.jhu.edu

Library of Congress Cataloging-in-Publication Data

Elder, D. Rose, 1952–
Why the Amish sing : songs of solidarity and identity / D. Rose Elder ;
foreword by Terry E. Miller.
    pages   cm. — (Young Center books in Anabaptist & Pietist studies)
Includes bibliographical references and index.
ISBN 978-1-4214-1465-2 (hardcover : alk. paper) —
ISBN 978-1-4214-1466-9 (electronic) — ISBN 1-4214-1465-1 (hardcover : alk. paper) —
ISBN 1-4214-1466-X (electronic) 1. Amish—Hymns—History and criticism. 2. Amish—
Music—History and criticism. 3. Amish—Social life and customs. I. Title.
ML3178.A45E43 2014
782.32'2973—dc23   2013046567

A catalog record for this book is available from the British Library.

Special discounts are available for bulk purchases of this book. For more information,
please contact Special Sales at 410-516-6936 or specialsales@press.jhu.edu.

Johns Hopkins University Press uses environmentally friendly book materials,
including recycled text paper that is composed of at least 30 percent
post-consumer waste, whenever possible.

Contents

*To listen to audio recordings of Amish singing,
please visit https://jhupbooks.press.jhu.edu/content/why-amish-sing.*

Foreword

For decades, the Amish have been one of America's most prominent "exotic others." Because they strictly keep to themselves and seek to maintain a distinct cultural identity, they have, by default, allowed others to define them. They have been unwilling to harness the commodification of their identity, giving non-Amish carte blanche to stereotype and exploit them: in the many Der Dutchman restaurants where hearty portions of starch, meat, and sugar are served; as the sellers of "made in China" Amish-style trinkets; on Amish tourist farms where buggy rides are offered; as well as in misunderstandings seen in the use of Dutch (rather than Deutsch) windmills, wooden shoes, and floral designs. This is partly the result of their own reticence to permit scholars access to their inner culture. This has been particularly true with regard to Amish singing, because much of it takes place in the context of worship, which is extremely private. That ethnomusicologist D. Rose Elder has been able to gain the trust of a major Amish community in Ohio and was allowed to document Amish singing in all its forms is a testament to her perseverance, sensitivity, and cultural knowledge.

Elder's study exemplifies classic ethnomusicology, a field that developed rapidly after World War II, when "the study of music" began to include the entire world as international travel increased. Ethnomusicologists traveled to wherever the music was being made and, because it was mostly oral performance, they had to create their own documentation through photographs, film/video, audio recordings, and interviews. Taking their cues from anthropology, field researchers often became participant-observers. Mantle Hood promoted the idea of bi-musicality, where researchers learned to perform the tradition they studied. Thus, ethnomusicology has long had a dual personality: studying music as an aspect of culture and studying music as a sonic phenomenon. Elder's study of Amish singing speaks to both.

Over many years, Elder built the relationships and trust that were necessary for her field work. Eventually, she was permitted to record a full range of song types, including those sung in church. Here she presents a comprehensive survey of Amish song types in context, describing the situations in which they were encountered and giving the singers a human side, even as they remain anonymous. She has transcribed the songs she recorded into staff notation so that readers can get an idea of how the Amish song world is constructed. Following the traditions of American folklore, she has classified the songs according to function and sentiment.

As ubiquitous as Amish culture is in several parts of the United States—especially northeast Ohio, central Ohio, eastern Pennsylvania, and central Indiana—few outsiders have ever heard Amish singing. Recordings other than those kept in well-guarded archives barely exist. There are no occasions where Amish singers present themselves to the public as other groups do, such as in folk festivals, international festivals, or special programs on NPR or PBS. For many other groups, church services are the natural sites to experience those cultures, because most church buildings are open to the public. This is not so with the Amish, since their congregations meet on a rotating basis in private homes instead of church buildings. They have schools, but these sit unmarked on country roads, and because they are private, outsiders may visit only by invitation. Elder was privileged to attend church services, enter schools, and visit private homes for her research.

The Amish have become idealized as old-fashioned, industrious craftsmen and farmers who remain close to the soil, eat whole foods, pollute but little, consume minimal amounts of energy, and take care of their families and communities. Some might see them as ideal Libertarians who depend on their community rather than the government. This stereotype is portrayed wherever merchants offer "Amish made" furniture, crafts, or even buildings. They are seen as the last bastions of old European hand craftsmanship. But when the Amish turn up among the general public, they sometimes exhibit perplexing traits. Young Amish men sometimes drive buggies through the countryside while blasting popular music from gigantic battery-powered amplifiers and speakers and occasionally behave as wildly as any non-Amish teens. Amish communities have their own share of problems, but they try to address them as much as possible with their own resources. Like the rest of us, they are sometimes self-contradictory and belie their idealized stereotypes.

The Amish experience disease, sadness, disappointment, betrayal, death, joy, abundance, poverty, discomfort, and uncertainty like everyone else. Many of these emotions and experiences are expressed in their songs. These songs, however austere and reserved, provide rare windows into the Amish soul. Their songs articulate their beliefs and perspectives on the world and their hope for eternal life. Their melodies and words reinforce their core beliefs about how to behave, how a community is organized and functions, what to believe about their place in the universe, and how to relate to one another. It is through song that the Amish tell one an-other—and potentially the rest of the world—who they are and what they have experienced. Tours of "Amish villages," buggy rides, and meals of meat, bread, and potatoes at a gigantic "Amish restaurant" show us little of the Amish soul or world view. Because the Amish write few confessional studies of themselves and rarely bare their souls to outsiders in novels, movies, or public lectures, their songs provide a wonderful opening into their world.

Elder's work therefore helps us not only to see the Amish as human be-ings like ourselves but to see ourselves through the Amish. Ironically, even as we have idealized Amish life, few non-Amish desire to live as they do. But there is no doubt that they deserve our respect for maintaining a de-manding alternative lifestyle and for preserving their dialect, their songs, and their sense of communal solidarity.

Terry E. Miller
Professor Emeritus of Ethnomusicology
Kent State University

Preface

Quilts and buggies. Uniform dress and an emphasis on hard work. One-room schoolhouses and barn raisings. Pacifism and gendered division of labor. That's what people generally know about the Amish. Curiosity about the Amish thrives, but most outsiders have scant awareness of the reality of Amish life and thought. What does it mean to be Amish? How do the Amish conduct their daily lives? What practices comprise their faith, and how do they maintain identities and values so different from the world around them?

From their early American home in Lancaster, Pennsylvania, to Middlefield or Holmes County, Ohio, to Nappanee, Indiana, and further west, north, and southward, the Amish phenomenon draws crowds. Legions of "English" (as the Amish call non-Amish people) arrive in Amish communities to sample "Amish" buggy rides, farm tours, cabinetry, home-cooked meals, quilts, and similar products.

Few tourists, however, get a chance to hear the Amish sing. Amish music remains largely an unexplored terrain in popular literature, and scholarly research has lagged. While musicologists, historians, and linguists have illuminated many facets of the hymnody of the *Ausbund* and the way it functions in Amish worship life (see appendix III), research on Amish music, infrequent in the past fifty years, continues to limit itself to the analysis, description, and notation of Amish church singing. This study attempts to address that lack of attention to the informal social and familial uses of music by looking at the many and diverse ways in which singing accompanies the activities of daily life in Amish communities.

Likewise, few studies consider the changes in Amish singing over the past hundred years. In this book, I seek to remedy these deficits by comparing the recordings and transcriptions of musicologists and Amish writers from the 1930s to the 1960s to current practice among the Old Order and New Order Amish in Wayne and Holmes Counties, Ohio. I place the songs and styles in their historical contexts and explain the role and purpose of singing in nourishing and nurturing Amish children to be Amish.

Although it is difficult to prove cause and effect between singing and the vitality of this group, the Amish themselves agree that music holds a significant position in their lives. Singing helps to create Amish attitudes and an Amish worldview. As an approved activity, singing occurs in nearly every setting of Amish life and frames all their rituals, from worship, baptism, communion, courtship, and weddings to funerals. It enlivens, improves, and sanctifies both routine and special events: road trips by buggy or hired van, daily school opening exercises or holiday programs given for parents and grandparents, youth group gatherings for forging bonds of friendship, "single girl" sings or men's sings for companionship and practicing the old hymn tunes. For many families, singing enriches daily routines of family prayer, rocking and soothing the perennial newborn, working in the garden, kitchen, barn, or other job site, and evenings relaxing on the porch. The corporate act of music-making stands at the center of Amish faith and life, urging me to document and discuss the singing of the Amish in all these social settings.

Also, music, like religion, can be a radicalizing force. Ancient songs that the Amish sing from their hymnal, the *Ausbund*, may at first sound stodgy and old-fashioned, especially to contemporary listeners accustomed to much faster, more rhythmic, and much shorter songs. However, many of the texts and melodies, written by martyrs in the sixteenth century, strengthened the ancestors of the Amish to give up everything—life, limb, status, and wealth—for their faith. Today, these same songs actively prepare Amish singers for resistance to the modern world, strange as that resistance may seem to outsiders. Amish hymnody serves to convict, convince, unite, and solace the believers as they struggle to learn and incorporate the words of faith that bring them closer to God.

We begin this study with an overview of Amish life and the role of singing in it, and then we move to a case study of a particular song, "Es sind zween Weg," and explore what it demonstrates about Amish singing styles, musical diversity, and conceptions of boundaries. In Part II, we focus on Amish singing in childhood and adolescence, with visits to Amish homes, schools, and youth sings. Part III investigates various aspects of Amish worship singing, and Part IV looks at songs for special occasions— weddings and funerals, miscellaneous events such as bus trips and holidays—as well as the future of Amish singing. All along the way, we focus particularly on Old Order and New Order Amish singing in Holmes and Wayne Counties, Ohio, with frequent references to more general Amish practices as well.

First, we start with a brief primer on Amish faith and practice. After examining the general contours of Amish life, we can narrow our lens to look specifically at Amish singing.

Acknowledgments

Writing a book requires a bevy of supporters. I would like to express my gratitude to my brilliant and driven spouse, Peter Rutkoff, who kept me going, and my kind and generous children, Autumn, April, Joshua, Burr, and Kathleen, for their creative ideas and steady, loving encouragement. To my parents, Dorothy and Fred Elder, who taught me perseverance and a love of music and religious thought, to Judy and Larry and Ramona, and to my wonderful friends, particularly Linda and Dan Houston, Lisa and Stu Shott, Dan Varisco and Najwa Adra, Patsy and Manny Stone, and my dream groupers, Linda, Mary, Dorothy, and Keith, goes my deep appreciation for their friendship and advice. Thanks to Donald Kraybill and George Kreps for their inspiration.

I want to give special thanks to all my Amish friends, particularly Jacob and Irma Beachy, Atlee and Mary Miller, Steve Miller, Jerry Miller, the Gingerichs, the Masts, and the Klines, for the generous gift of their time, willingness to talk with me and sing for me, and for reading and commenting on my manuscripts. As requested, I have invented names for other interviewees to protect their anonymity.

Several student assistants, Autumn Stewart-Zimmerman, Andrea Lucas, Patrice Trudell, and Esther Diehl, deserve thanks and kudos for their contributions to the project. Thanks to Martina Machniach and Julia Naderer for German translation assistance. Thanks to Greg Nicholl, Sara Cleary, Deborah Bors, my editing and marketing support at Johns Hopkins University Press, and Valerie Weaver-Zercher, who provided developmental editing. And, last, this work owes a measure of credit to the National Endowment for Humanities and the Ohio State University's Ohio Agricultural Research and Development Center for the funding each provided early in my research.

Some parts of chapters 2–7 were published previously in an earlier form in the following:

"O Gott Vater, Wir Loben Dich": Amish Childhood Singing Forges Commitment to God and Community. *Pennsylvania Mennonite Heritage* 27:1(Jan):8–25 (2004).

"Es Sind Zween Weg": Singing Amish Children into the Faith Community. *Cultural Analysis: An Interdisciplinary Forum on Folklore and Popular Culture* 2:39–67 (2001).

'Shlof, Bubeli, Shlof': Amish Songs to Grow By. Proceedings of Serving Amish and Anabaptist Communities, Tri-State Extension Services, Walnut Creek, Ohio, 28–30 March (2001). Used with permission of Ohio State University Extension, outreach arm of the College of Food, Agricultural, and Environmental Sciences, 2120 Fyffe Road, Columbus, OH, 43210.

PART I

Amish Life and Song

CHAPTER 1

Who Are the Amish?

Bedenke, Mensch! das Ende,	*Consider, human, the end,*
Bedenke deinen Tod,	*Consider your death.*
Der Tod kommt oft behende;	*Death often comes quickly.*
Der heute frisch und rot,	*Today you are healthy and ruddy,*
Kann morgen und geschwinder	*Tomorrow and even sooner,*
Hinweg gestorben sein;	*You, poor wretch, are suddenly dead;*
Darum bilde dir, o Sünder!	*Every day, sinner,*
Ein täglich Sterben ein.	*Imagine yourself as dying.*

—*Eine Unparteiische Liedersammlung* (1892/1999)

Mary's back is turned away from the door when I enter the schoolroom. Clustered around their young teacher, five ten- to twelve-year-old girls murmur softly, intensely, conspiratorially. Mary is dressed, as they are, in a solid-colored dress. Her headcovering is white; theirs, black. Half a dozen other children, throughout the expanse of the high-ceilinged, century-old, one-room schoolhouse, turn to gaze curiously at me. Another rainy day in Ohio confines all the young scholars inside. Those at their desks play tic-tac-toe, read, or assemble puzzles. I hear a ball banging in a jerky rhythm; in the basement, some of the boys are playing dodgeball and ping-pong.

Mary welcomes me with a warm, genuine smile and draws me into her circle. Respectfully, the children fall silent. Forewarned of my visit by her cousin who teaches at the school I visited yesterday, Mary is garrulous. "I've been teaching for five years, and I learn something new every year," she tells me. Mary inquires about my contacts within the Amish community, and we chat about people we both know. Very soon it is 8:30, time to take attendance—twenty-nine students with three teachers, which includes one for a special education group of four meeting in a back corner, partitioned off by a chest-high screen. The formal school day opens with singing. "We sing in German on Fridays," Mary says, and hesitates. "Is that okay?" I assure her that it's fine with me.

Junior serves as the first of the morning's two *Vorsingers*, or songleaders. He chooses "Es sind zween Weg," from the *Liedersammlung*, a songbook frequently used among the Amish. After an enthusiastic rendition of Junior's song, the second *Vorsinger*, Roman, announces his selection, "Bedenke Mensch, das Ende." The group happily joins him, but I cringe at the grim meaning of the text (Musical Example 1.1).[1]

2. Be - den - ke, Mensch! das En - de, Be - den - ke das Ge - richt;
Es__ müs-sen al - le__ Stän-de vor Je- sus Un- ge__ sicht:

Musical Example 1.1. "Bedenke Mensch, das Ende," Holmes County school (1999).
Translation: (*verse 2*) *Consider, human, the end, consider the judgment;*
Everyone—you, too—has to come before Jesus:
No one is spared. Everyone has to show up
To receive the reward earned in his [or her] lifetime.

Roman sings as loudly as all the rest of the children combined. Not all the children sing on pitch, but I hear a musicality to the line. The phrases flow. With their young teachers, the children thus joyfully place themselves along the vector of history, tradition, and faith that stretches back to the sixteenth century. Through music, they mine the repository of memory that was shaped by their ancestors and that remains a touchstone of their identity.

This leads us to the central claim of this study: singing accompanies many everyday events in Amish life and, through its frequent and central role in community life, becomes an essential vessel through which identity, memory, devotion, and culture are transmitted. We will turn to the role of singing in Amish life in chapter 2, but we should first examine the history of the Amish and some facets of their common life. A rudimentary understanding of their cultural and religious practices will illuminate the ways in which the Amish form their lives by and through their singing.

Overview of the Amish

The Amish derive their name from their first leader, Jacob Amman, who was born in 1644.[2] Amman led a splinter group away from the Swiss Brethren Anabaptists (later known as Mennonites), who themselves had broken from the Swiss Reformed pastor Ulrich Zwingli's church in Zürich in 1525. At its core, the Anabaptists emphasized the importance of adult baptism and a church that lived apart from the popular culture of the larger world. After years of persecution and forced diaspora throughout Europe, Amman's group emerged in the 1690s as a renewal group within the Swiss Anabaptists and in the Alsace region of present-day France. Amman and his followers were concerned about what they considered increasing waywardness and conformity to the world among the traditional Swiss Brethren churches. In 1693, Amman led an offshoot branch that soon became known as Amish. Under his leadership, the Amish church emphasized a stricter shunning of excommunicated members, greater separation from the state churches, and practicing communion twice a year. Following the model of Jesus, they included footwashing in the communion service. In the 1730s, some Amish immigrants followed Mennonite pioneers and sought asylum in religiously tolerant Pennsylvania. Successful settlements insured a steady flow of Amish to the North American continent in two waves, between 1736 and 1770 and again in the years 1815–1860. In the New World, clusters of Amish families collaborated to support and encourage each other in faithful living.[3]

In the twenty-first century, Amish people live in thirty different states and in the Canadian province of Ontario. They have established more than two thousand local congregations in some 470 geographical communities.[4] The Amish call their local congregations church districts. Each district consists of twenty to forty families living in an area with geographical boundaries. Members of the district select and ordain a bishop, two ministers, and a deacon from among their ranks to provide leadership. The Amish gather in their homes for worship services every other Sunday because they do not have church buildings. When the number of families grows too large to meet comfortably in a home, the district will divide and form two new districts.

Outsiders frequently, and inaccurately, speak of "the Amish" as though they are one group. Each district belongs to an affiliation or subgroup of the Amish. The Amish has differentiated into more than forty different affiliations in North America. Each has its own distinctive set of regulations and practices. There are nearly a dozen different affiliations in the large Holmes County, Ohio, settlement, which actually spans several counties.[5] Affiliations range from the very conservative Swartzentrubers, who live austere lives without indoor plumbing and rarely interact with non-Amish, to progress-minded groups who use land lines or cell phones, operate sizable businesses, and interact freely with outsiders. Nevertheless, all Amish groups drive horses and buggies for their primary mode of transportation. They speak the Pennsylvania Dutch dialect and wear distinctive clothing that separates them from modern American culture.

One Old Order Amish woman acknowledges the schisms: "We don't like to identify ourselves like that, New Order or Old Order. But on Sunday mornings there are buggies from five different orders that go down this road. They go every which way. There are the New Order Tobe, Old Tobe, Andy Weaver . . . They broke away from us . . . Swartzentruber, and ours. The Tobe broke away from the Swartzentrubers, but they got too ingrown. Now they commune with us and intermarry."[6]

The Amish experience great diversity, even within affiliations, because they believe theological authority ultimately rests in the individual church district. Thus, neighboring districts even in the same affiliation may have different regulations. Still, many non-Amish people familiar with one Amish community incorrectly assume that every Amish group looks and acts exactly the same. This brings us to the Amish in Holmes County, Ohio, the primary area of this study.

The Amish in Ohio

In 1808, Jacob Miller, the first Amish settler, arrived in Ohio. Jonas Stutzman, called "Der Weiss" because of his habit of dressing in white, soon followed and settled in Holmes County in 1809 (figure 1.1). The relatively isolated farmland of northeastern Ohio provided fertile ground for growing and preserving their sixteenth-century style religious community. By 1862, the Ohio settlement had gained enough strength and voice to organize and host a national meeting of Amish leaders called the *Diener-Versammlungen*. These national gatherings, which occurred virtually every year from 1862 through 1878, eventually produced a major schism, with the most traditional churches emerging as the Old Order

Figure 1.1 Ohio Historical Marker: Jonas Stutzman, First Amishman in Holmes County. "Jonas Stutzman 'Der Weiss' 1-31-1788—10-18-1871. Jonas Stutzman, from Somerset County, Pennsylvania, came to this site in 1809 to clear land for farming and to build a log home for his family. He was the first permanent settler in the eastern portion of what would in 1825 become Holmes County. Jonas and his wife Magdalena Gerber Stutzman were of the Amish faith—descendants from a group of strict Protestant Anabaptists with origins in Switzerland and Holland and dating from the 16th-century Protestant Reformation. Some of their beliefs, including separation of church and state, refusal to take oaths, pacifism, and believer's baptism, were perceived as threats to the state church and government. Persecuted by both the Catholics and the Protestants, Anabaptists migrated and some came to the New World, many at the invitation of Pennsylvania's William Penn. The Stutzman's and other early Amish pioneer settlers— Millers, Hershbergers, Hochstetlers, Masts, Troyers, and Schrocks—founded here what has become the largest Amish settlement in North America. *Ohio Bicentennial Commission, The Longaberger Company, German Cultural Museum of Walnut Creek, The Ohio Historical Society 2002.*" Photograph by Nathan Crook, 23 October 2013.

Amish and the more progress-oriented ones becoming Amish Mennonites who gradually joined various Mennonite groups.

Ohio has a history of birthing and nurturing new religious groups. From early nineteenth-century America, when the religious fervor of western New York spilled over into Ohio, the newly established state provided a haven for more than twenty-one religious, reform, and utopian communities. Affordable land prices, easier access through the transportation routes of the Erie Canal and National Road, and a tolerance for idealism and diversity positioned Ohio for rapid development, swelling the population from 231,000 in 1810 to 938,000 in 1830.[7] Although the Amish did not specifically seek to create a heaven on earth in a true sense, their emphasis on godly living and separation from the world set in motion their search for a more isolated territory than eastern Pennsylvania. The gently sloping hills of Tuscarawas, Holmes, and Wayne Counties drew and nourished their communities with natural bounty.

In their home in the growing Holmes County settlement, the Amish pursued hard work and mutual concern, values similar to those of their non-Amish neighbors. Both worked, struggled, and experienced joy in creating handmade quilts, tending tidy gardens, planting straight corn-rows, singing to pass the time in cart or buggy, attending church and saying prayers as a family, and raising their children strictly without "sparing the rod." They respected each other's privacy but called on each other in times of need. They were separate but equal in love of God, showing charity toward neighbors, living by the rhythms of the land, and enjoying simple pleasures. Throughout the twentieth century, mechanization, social change, and migration to cities widened the gulf between the Amish and their neighbors, but the two groups maintained courteous interactions and friendships.

Since 1970, the Holmes County Amish settlement has experienced rapid and unprecedented change. Land prices skyrocketed and tourism expanded rapidly, creating traffic snarls in small towns. Amish tourism in Holmes County surpassed Cedar Point Amusement Park as Ohio's number one attraction. For some, peace of mind seemed a distant memory. The pros and cons of this development led one Amish bishop to observe, "Because of the traffic, we only take our buggies into town on Monday and Tuesday mornings." Then he quips, "On the positive side, we don't have to leave town to be missionaries. Just open the door and they're there!"

For the Ohio Amish, these changes and choices have challenged their self-sufficiency and long-standing traditions. Yet they have grown and prospered as never before. By 2013, Ohio's Holmes County settlement, with 32,000 Amish, made up nearly 12 percent of the 275,000 Amish in North America. The Amish described in this book belong to several affiliations that reside in the settlement centered in Wayne and Holmes Counties.

Economic Life

The Amish across North America maintain a network of close-knit communities, thriving, well-kept homesteads and farms, and small-scale, Amish-owned and -staffed businesses in the midst of a sometimes hostile—albeit sometimes alluring—surrounding culture. The Amish still affirm a rural lifestyle sustained by hard work, conservative values, and close parent-child relationships that helps to preserve their "plain" way of living. Although many of them consider farming the best occupation, fewer than ten percent of the Amish in the Holmes County region receive their primary income from farming. For the last thirty-five years, the number of Amish farms has steadily decreased, because affordable land was not available and because of the low investment and high profitability of small businesses. Some members resisted this change and have moved to more remote areas to find farmland. But others are content to remain and devise other ways of making a living, such as furniture making, equipment manufacturing, carpentry, greenhouses, horticulture, and landscaping. One man started a printing press, another a hardware store that loans chainsaws and other tools. Some Amish businesses, such as blacksmiths and fabric shops, cater to the needs within the Amish community. Women sew quilts at home, work in shops, or provide childcare or clean homes for non-Amish neighbors. Married women usually work at home. Families grow large vegetable gardens and sell produce in family roadside markets. An increasing number of families earn their income by raising produce to sell to grocery chains. For example, at the vegetable auction in Mt. Hope, Ohio, visitors see semi—tractor trailers adorned with the logos of major grocery stores. Students of Amish life have researched whether farming is necessary for the continuation of the Amish culture. They have observed that, despite the rapid downturn in family farming, the number of people in the Amish community continues to double about every twenty years.[8]

One grave concern that older Amish people deliberate is whether economic openness and entrepreneurship will undermine the mutual dependence that characterizes Amish culture. "If a community is to survive, it must structure the interaction of its members to strengthen ways of being and knowing which support community," maintains social scientist Stephen Marglin. "It will have to constrain the market when the market undermines the community."[9] As interdependence weakens, Marglin predicts that community solidarity will decline and more members will defect from the community. One bishop advises that this is the reason that Amish leaders discourage large businesses.

Family Life

Amish daily life revolves around the routines of work and family, punctuated with planting and harvesting, disinfecting the barn for a new batch of poultry, or spring housecleaning. Mothers and daughters often work together on major tasks, even after daughters have their own families. One summer morning, four generations—great-aunt, mother, three sisters, and two granddaughters (who ride tricycles on the gravel drive)—are preserving endless bushels of peaches. At a nearby homestead, two small tots follow their father into the garden to pick beans. Down the road, two sisters are mowing the lawn. Buggy rides to the store or to visit neighbors, walks, baseball or volleyball games, and rocking on the porch swing round out the days.

The normative Amish family remains quite large, with typically six to eight children. One Amish woman mentions that her neighbor had fourteen babies over a twenty-year period. She insists that this mother continues to be unfailingly kind to all and that her children have become very nice, well-adjusted people. Even as family size decreases in the dominant culture, Amish parents continue to have more than five children, a few families as many as sixteen.

The use of contraceptives is not acceptable, but some groups find ways to limit fertility. One Amish woman volunteered, "As the bishop put it, he's not in favor of birth control; he's in favor of self-control. On the other hand, when you go back in genealogy or relationship books, children were generally born two years apart. They were breastfed and I think that's probably how God intended it to be. I don't think a woman was meant to have a baby every year."[10] One Old Order Amish woman in her sixties discloses, "My younger sister had eleven children and as of today has 105 grand- and great-grand children."

Large numbers of children function as an asset to Amish families. Unlike in mainstream American homes, where raising children means costly college educations, music lessons and sports clubs, a never-ending stream of clothes in the latest fashion, or endless consumer and leisure expenses, Amish parents do not focus on the financial burden but on the blessing of having children. Of course, having children ensures the well-being of Amish parents as they grow older. Amish adults prepare for their retirement years but also depend on their children to care for them if they become disabled.

Producing children only begins the process of growing the community. These children must, as young adults, elect to stay within the community and take up their responsibilities as members and, probably, parents themselves. To this end, Amish parents and grandparents model a strong work ethic, self-discipline, interdependency, and selflessness.

Amish Identity

Identity formation in Amish communities mirrors the process observed in other cultures. An individual's identity is a complex combination of genetic endowments (nature) and personal experiences (nurture). Psychologists have found that an infant's personality is enduring. Fussy babies tend to make fussy adults; placid babies, adults with sunny dispositions. But, experiences with others, such as the parenting a child receives and interactions with siblings, also have their influences. As one author explains, "The self-contradiction—a Westerner would call it paradox—[is] that we only acquire our own identity by imitating others."[11] Relatives and friends apply "procedures of measuring, surveillance, and correction," writes Michel Foucault.[12] The individual also measures himself against internalized standards of what it means to be a good, successful, honest child.

The "ideal" personality that the Amish value is that of a "quiet, friendly, responsible, conscientious, devoted worker, patient with detail and routine, loyal, considerate and concerned with others' feelings even when they're in the wrong."[13] Amish parents have the responsibility of nurturing these qualities in their children. Although they believe that children are born with sinful natures, Amish parents also trust that their children

are teachable and will become loving, dedicated people in the proper environment.[14] The Amish reinforce this "ideal self" through basic community
activities—a close, intense family life, regular patterns of visitation with
opportunities to observe each other in home settings, worship gatherings,
collective youth activities, and education in private schools.

Amish parents require honesty and obedience. In the May 2001 issue
of *Family Life*, an Amish periodical, "Abner and His Cookies" tells about a
boy stealing cookies from the cupboard and getting his finger caught in a
mousetrap. His mother commiserates with Abner about his sore finger but
tells him, "You will have to be punished. I'm sure that after this you will
think twice before disobeying."[15]

Teen years can be troublesome times in many cultures. Mainstream
teens struggle with many powerful and puzzling influences, intense hor-
monal changes, higher-level thoughts with accompanying intense self-
reflection, and social pressures as they make life choices of career and
mate.[16] They struggle to discover "Who am I?" and "What do I stand for?"
Amish youth encounter these same issues, but Amish teens' identities are
less diffuse because most accept their limited choices for education, work,
marriage partners, and lifestyle.[17] Wisely, Amish adults understand that
certain Amish teenagers wrestle longer with identity issues. They allow
teens some latitude to experiment during *Rumspringa*, a time period that
has gained popular attention thanks to the well-publicized excesses of a
few Amish youth. Still, most Amish youth freely choose to join the church
as adults; currently, nearly 90% of Amish youth ultimately accept the
Amish way and elect to be baptized, the highest rate since the 1930s.[18]

According to psychologist Eric Erickson, identity formation in middle-
aged and older adults is often characterized by generativity and integrity,
with continuing growth and a sense of satisfaction of a life well-lived—or
stagnation and despair, with a feeling of regret that life has passed them
by.[19] Although a few admit that they do not feel they fit well within their
community, well-socialized Amish adults enjoy working, exchanging
ideas, collaborating with their neighbors, and nurturing contented children and grandchildren. They feel a secure sense of fulfillment in their
faithfulness to God and community.

Mutual Aid

Most likely, the feelings of security arise from the Amish emphasis on mutual reliance. The Amish reluctance to accept telephones without any restrictions rests on their insistence that face-to-face encounters increase mutual reliance and respect. They believe that people must care, support, and treat each other kindly and honestly as human beings and not objects. Further, they express that face-to-face interaction facilitates those relational qualities. Nevertheless, the increase in cell phone use in some of the affiliations attests to their growing use of technology in the last decade.

Because the Amish practice mutual support, they do not pay into the Social Security system, nor do they typically receive government aid. In the face of hardship, members of the community rally to help each other. The quintessential Amish barn raisings feature coordinated teams of men building a barn from start to finish in one day while women cook and serve the hungry workers hearty meals. If someone needs expensive surgery and extended hospitalization, members contribute. During one of my conversations with an Amish man, his neighbor's cows escaped. The man stopped in the middle of our conversation, pulled on his high-topped rubber boots, and plodded across the field to herd them back without a backward glance.

The Amish not only raise funds to help a neighbor in need, but they also participate in general relief efforts. Some Amish construction teams helped with rebuilding after Florida's Hurricane Andrew in 1996 and Louisiana's Hurricane Katrina in 2005. In Wayne County, Ohio, one Amish group regularly builds a home for a working-class family in partnership with the local Habitat for Humanity. Groups of women sew quilts and send them to missions in developing countries. Youth visit non-Amish residents in nursing home facilities, jails, and hospitals or teach in Old Colony Mennonite schools in Mexico. The Amish are aware of the world outside their community and feel compelled to pitch in. "We are the light of the world," one Amish person told me. "All Christians should live the godly life and testify by their 'walk.'"[20] This caring and cooperation was learned in small rural schools.

Amish Schools

Many older Amish people have fond memories of the one-room public schools they attended. One great-grandfather talks about his non-Amish teacher, whose breadth and depth of knowledge inspired his classmates for all eight years of their schooling. The consolidation of public school districts changed this pattern. Rather than applauding the dominant culture's plan to expand rural children's educational opportunities, the Amish experienced distress as they realized that the loss of local control and busing their children to distant schools would undermine the ability of Amish parents to supervise their children's education.

Even though the government required them to pay property taxes to support public schools, many Amish communities decided that they would open private parent-directed schools. The traditional one-room school suited their needs because it was local. In some areas of the country, Amish parents purchased one-room public schools that had closed. In other states, Amish parents were jailed for prohibiting their children from entering high school. Finally, in 1972, the U.S. Supreme Court in *Wisconsin v. Yoder* determined that Amish children could terminate their formal education at eighth grade. By 2012, nearly two thousand one- or two-room Amish schools, funded, built, and maintained by parents without government aid, were functioning in North America. Currently, nearly all of the Amish children in Pennsylvania and Ohio attend private schools for their formal education, which consists of grades one to eight. In addition, a few public elementary schools, including some in Holmes County, serve Amish children almost exclusively.[21]

To organize an Amish school, three to five fathers form a school board, which approves all school activities. It selects desired playground equipment, chooses schoolbooks, and hires or fires teachers. Keeping good, experienced teachers can be a problem. A survey of fifty Amish schools listed in *Blackboard Bulletin*, an Amish publication for educators, shows that many Amish teachers leave the occupation after two or three years to get married or to find an easier job. One young schoolteacher explained that teaching eight grades is too difficult, so she left to teach a single grade in a local Mennonite school; she married the next year. One middle-aged Amish man admits that his contract was not renewed when he was a young teacher because a parent caught him listening to a baseball game on a transistor radio. He violated the expectation of being a good role model. Needless to say, parents keep close oversight over their school. Young teachers feel the pressure of fierce scrutiny by parents and church leaders.

Indeed, Amish schooling may have replaced the family farm as one of the most important factors in keeping Amish children within the community. Their schools limit children's contact with outsiders while they develop friendships with cousins and neighbors that knit them tightly to the community. Within the simple confines of a school for twenty-five to thirty students, many things add up to an agreeable, informal pattern of socialization: simple pleasures of twice-daily games of baseball with a beloved and gloved teacher in the outfield, a massive chunk of cheese available to all on the back shelf in the classroom, the teacher's full attention for a small group of two or three learners for fifteen minutes at a time throughout the day, and warming up around the potbelly stove while chatting with friends in Pennsylvania Dutch, their community's language.

Language and Lifestyle

Many Amish children first learn English in school. Pennsylvania Dutch, the primary language Amish children use for family, church, and all intra-Amish conversation, fosters a distinctive ethnic identity. Maintaining that language solidifies the group and sharply sets the boundary of difference with the outside world. Andrea Fishman suggests, "Bilingualism cannot be supported without biculturalism, awareness of one's heritage, identification with it and freedom to express this identification in a natural and uninhibited manner."[22]

Two languages, two cultures. Amish children learn that they owe allegiance to their group and must adopt their parents' lifestyle choices. In addition to building identity, a language serves as a way of knowing the world. Some ideas and concepts resist translation from one language to another precisely because language is not just a way of communicating an experience but an orientation to a total way of life, a way of perceiving and interpreting the world. Ethnic communities in the United States find that when they drift away from speaking their native languages, their children blend into the mainstream society. The adherence to their language, paired with intentional community living, helps the Amish remain separate from the dominant American education, mass culture, politics, and economy.[23]

The Amish also resist the forces of assimilation by maintaining common dress, simple living, and the discipline of the *Ordnung*, the community's agreed-upon rules for behavior. As applied to the Amish, "simple" means plain or unornamented, denoting an opposition to a fancy, ostentatious lifestyle. The Amish are not simple-minded or simplistic about their lifestyle and technological choices; they set limits, seek to be practical, and pay close attention to the stewardship of resources.

Publications

Amish presses that print periodicals and books to inform, encourage, and connect Amish households enrich Amish life. Three monthly magazines published by Pathway Publishers in Aylmer, Ontario, address various Amish concerns.[24] *Blackboard Bulletin* shows teachers how to encourage student learning—"Go slowly and do your best"—how to maintain order and discipline, and why school singing is an important part of the school day. *Young Companion,* for teens and twenty-year-olds, talks about both finding a Christian partner and being happy while single. Contributors send opinion essays, short stories, and poetry to *Family Life,* a magazine with Bible puzzles, stories, recipes, and health information.

In Holmes County, Ohio, *The Budget* publishes news of Amish families, out-of-town visitors, marriages, and arrivals of new babies. Published in Walnut Creek, Ohio, *Bird Enthusiast* opens up the secrets and beauty of the natural world. *Die Botschaft* and *The Diary,* published in eastern Pennsylvania, are papers filled with news of friends and relatives written by hundreds of Amish scribes in local communities in many states. Additionally, some Amish read local newspapers, news magazines, and periodicals related to hunting and fishing or occupations such as furniture making. Amish people also take advantage of the opportunity to borrow books from public libraries and in some cases bookmobiles stocked with Amish preferences.

Singing

Most significantly for this study, the Amish accompany many aspects of their worship, work, and pleasure time with singing. Amish adults swaddle their children in music. Parents sing nursery songs to comfort their young, to accompany their work in the kitchen or garden with babies and toddlers nearby, and to relax on the porch after a long day. Older siblings sing songs learned in school or sometimes harmonize on gospel songs. Babies attend bi-weekly, home-based worship services of more than three hours, with at least a third of the time spent in singing *Ausbund* songs from their premier hymnbook.

The quintessential music of the Amish, the *Ausbund* is a repository of sixteenth-century martyr's sermons in song. These connect the Amish to founders of the faith who wrote and sang in prison cells as they awaited their deaths. Giving witness to individual sacrifice and suffering, hymns in the *Ausbund* have been set to pre-existing tunes, probably folksongs, and preserved without musical notation. We examine these *Ausbund* songs in more detail in chapter 8.

As a rule, parents who sing raise children who engage more frequently in singing, but nearly all Amish people relate that singing is a very important part of their lives. One Amish man tilts his head back and reminisces, "My parents, five brothers, two sisters, and I sat on the porch every evening singing gospel songs in harmony."[25] Another mentions rocking his baby boys hour upon hour and singing old church hymns. One woman became wistful as she remembered her mother's singing while she performed household chores.

Even though the Amish only rarely discuss their singing, they value it as an important part of their culture. One Amish woman reports, "We sing while we work. Automatically children will sing, even before they can carry a tune. You just naturally sing with children. Since we don't have radio or tapes, we just do a lot of singing."[26] In one survey, more than 80 percent of 56 Amish adults interviewed in Wayne and Holmes Counties said that singing was important in their families, and 30 percent said that they sing two or more hours a day.[27]

Singing dovetails with the rest of Amish life to sustain culture, maintain identity, and resist or negotiate outside forces. It comforts, instructs, and unites. We will look at more ways that Amish singing functions in chapter 2, but we should first examine its connection to the spiritual and religious life of Amish communities.

Spirituality and Religion

For the Amish, all of life is a sacred journey. Even so, the rituals they perform set boundaries between everyday life and the more sacred. At home, they bless meals with prayer before and after eating. Many families engage in daily family Bible reading and prayer from *Christenpflicht* (Christian Duty), a devotional book first published in 1787.[28] Children silently pray a German blessing before going to sleep. Sunday worship occurs every other week. Other special worship occasions include baptism services, when young adults join the church. Twice-yearly communion services, ordinations, weddings, and funeral ceremonies are other important religious gatherings. The Amish neither baptize nor christen infants, but when new babies arrive, friends visit the family, welcoming the newborn and bringing practical gifts for the mother.

Preserving the tradition of holding worship services in the home, barn, or shop, families take turns hosting the gathering of 75 to 150 people once or twice a year. Each local district holds church services every other Sunday. On their "off" or "visiting" Sunday, families hitch up the horses, hop in the buggy, and call on their neighbors or go to another district's worship service to hear a different preaching style. Members of New Order congregations often hold Sunday school meetings on their off Sundays. Regardless of their particular Amish affiliation, visiting is nearly as important as worshipping.

All human cultures have developed religious practices, generally paired with sung expression. Through symbols, religious practices offer, preach, and teach patience, endurance, and courage for negotiating life's challenges. Symbol systems imbue ordinary events such as eating (in the Christian Holy Eucharist), sweating (in the Navajo Curing Ways), and breathing (in Buddhist practice) with supernatural meaning. These bring lucidity and a sense of order to the chaos inherent in life, thereby relieving human distress.

The Amish are no exception. They face the usual human trials and rely on their faith to help them cope and flourish. Anthropologist Clifford Geertz writes that life events that cause cognitive, physical, and moral discomfort or unease produce an existential anxiety, which pushes human societies to develop religion. Religion serves as "a system of symbols which acts to establish powerful, persuasive, and long-lasting moods and motivations in [people] by formulating conceptions of a general order of existence and clothing these conceptions with such an aura of factuality that the moods and motivations seem uniquely realistic."[29] Reflecting on Geertz's work, sociologist Patrick McNamara proposes that religion undergirds a social group by fulfilling four functions, the explanatory, validating, psychologically-reinforcing, and integrative functions (table 1.1).[30]

Table 1.1. McNamara's four functions of religion

Function	Role	Example
Explanatory	Offers insight into worthy questions	"Why do children suffer?"
Validating	Confirms institutions, values, goals	"Contentment is my delight."
Psychologically reinforcing	Provides security amid fear about random events	"God numbers the hairs on your head."
Integrative	Unites customs in overall design	"I am created in God's image and born to serve the Lord."

Source: Geertz, "Religion as a Cultural System," 14–17.

Often-used Amish songs reflect each of these four functions. The hymn that Roman chose in the opening narrative of this chapter, "Bedenke Mensch, das Ende," epitomizes the struggle of the Amish faith and the means, methods, and outcomes of the Amish socialization process. When Amish children sing "Bedenke Mensch, das Ende" in school, they are learning the basic tenets of their faith (Musical Example 1.2).

Be den ke, Mensch, das En - de! Be-den-ke dein-en Tod. Der Tod kommt oft be

hen - de Der heu - te frisch und rot. Kann mor-gen und ge schwin-der hin

weg ge-stor-ben sein, Da-rum bild dir o Sün- der! Ein täg lich Ster-ben ein.

Musical Example 1.2. "Bedenke Mensch, das Ende," Holmes County school (2002).
Translation: (verse 1) *Think, human, about the end, Think about your death.*
Death often comes quickly. One who is fresh and red,
Can tomorrow and sooner, be suddenly dead;
Therefore, imagine you, O sinner, as daily dying.

In both this variation and the version provided at the opening of the chapter, "Bedenke Mensch" provides an excellent example of the link between religion and singing in an Amish context. We should look at the song through the lens of McNamara's four functions of religion.

The explanatory function of religion. In its explanatory function, religion supplies insight into life's toughest questions: "Why?" "Why do we live the way we do?" and "Why do we suffer?" Religion offers strength of purpose, the recognition that "events are not just there and happen, but they have meaning and happen because of that meaning."[31]

In "Bedenke Mensch, das Ende," Amish children learn that their actions have consequences, and they gain insight into questions about suffering. Suffering is one way the Amish know they are on the right track. Rehearsing modern examples of persecution, such as conscientious objectors being exposed to hepatitis for medical studies or handcuffed to jail bars, continues this trend.[32] If they are faithful to God now, despite harassment, God will care for them throughout eternity. The dominant themes of this song hold special importance in the Amish belief system. Being faithful in mundane matters, yielding to God, and preparing for the inevitability of death and prophesied judgment will result in rescue from eternal punishment and obtain for them an eternal home with God. Thus, the song assists in explaining the humanly inexplicable, a central function of religion itself.

The validating function of religion. Second, in its validating function, religion confirms a society's basic institutions, values, and goals. Singing, in the case of the Amish, smoothly carries out that function. The Amish child sings about farming chores, staying on the narrow path, and relying on God for salvation. Amish song texts illustrate this point. In 1819, Daniel Schwartzentruber recorded these lyrics in his son's ledger: "Contentment is my delight. / All else I leave behind / And love and love and love contentment. / When all misfortunes spring forth roaring / And all stars in heaven are rolling, / Still will I trust my God. / Oh, beloved soul, be content / With whatever heaven has granted / And love and love and love contentment."[33]

Amish schoolchildren in the twenty-first century sing, "I was made in His likeness. / I was born to serve the Lord." The lifestyle that Amish parents choose facilitates an acceptance of the vagaries of human existence. Children learn from their parents to lean on God and the extended family. Moreover, their rural, mostly agrarian lifestyle thrives on cooperation and humility rather than on competition and pride of achievement. Singing "Bedenke Mensch, das Ende" reinforces this reality, as well as the reality of death, and expresses the goal of preparing children to be good community members of earth and heaven. In a wider society that considers many aspects of Amish life old-fashioned or untenable, Amish singing helps to validate the specific values and goals of the community.

The psychologically-reinforcing function of religion. Third, religion offers security in an unpredictable, even arbitrary, world during times of up-heaval.[34] Religious beliefs prepare the worshipper for the eventuality of death and offer solace. "Bedenke Mensch," while its words may sound bleak or foreboding to outsiders' ears, provides a solid and even comfort-ing reminder of eternal life past the grave.

Few events could be more difficult emotionally and psychologically than burying a child. Amish extended families may experience child death due to farming or buggy accidents, fires related to the use of kero-sene lamps and wood stoves, and genetically inherited diseases as a result of patterns of endogamy. At a funeral for a child, the Amish repeat hymn texts that direct the community to recognize that God makes the decisions of life and death and emphasize that their children ultimately belong to God. One graveside hymn at the funeral of a child comforts the attendees, "Even though it is very painful to us, / We must yet call it good / When the Lord takes our children / Because they are his heirs."[35]

On a basic level, Amish children learn to live by the *Ordnung*. They be-come responsible to each other and understand that as adults they may be censored or even shunned if they do not live up to the *Ordnung*. Sociologist John Hostetler observes, "Secular man searches for patterns and meaning in history, religious man does not need to; he knows the world is orderly and is so ordered by God."[36] The order and predictability of the Amish faith offer safety and direction, and the songs of Amish life assist in build-ing that sense of security, too.

The integrative function of religion. Last, religion integrates or unites cus-toms and beliefs into a cohesive design. Like their singing, Amish religion is largely unselfconscious. In 1930, one Amish bishop, Daniel E. Mast, wrote a blessing of the faithful in "The Duty of Children and Parents, Salvation Full and Free": "God's word is read and revered, as a preserving balm of the soul. God is magnified with reading, song and prayer, and all the heavenly hosts rejoice over the spiritual prosperity of such a family, cleansed from her sins, and the souls washed in the blood of the Lamb. Hallelujah! Amen."[37] A hymn favorite, "Gott ist die Liebe," reverberates with a blessing, insisting on the good will and love of God for each person (Musical Example 1.3).

While "Bedenke Mensch" emphasizes the sinfulness of each, "Gott ist

Gott ist die Lie - be. Gott ist die   Lie - be. Gott ist die Lie - be. Ich liebe auch mich.

Musical Example 1.3. "Gott ist die Liebe." Source: John J. Overholt, *Erweckungs Lieder*, 19.
Translation: *God is love, He loves me, too.*

die Liebe" proclaims freedom from sin and guilt when one asks forgiveness. It celebrates the freedom to choose to comply with God's will. The
Amish rely on a simple, consistent religious system that integrates a range
of practices and beliefs.

In summary, religious practices offer believers the comfort and security
that their reliance on God's promises will please God. Belief backed by
appropriate, godly action enables the individual and community to endure
trials and to celebrate triumphs. Moreover, Amish children learn through
daily experience and human example the meaning of being Amish.

This circles us back to the core claim of this study: that singing plays a
critical role in building and sustaining Amish identity. Corporate singing,
in the many manifestations that we examine in this book, forms an essential transaction in the process of passing on religious and cultural goods
to younger generations of Amish people. Amish singing is not simply the
emblem of a static culture. To maintain their identity and integrity, cultures have to adapt. While remaining constant in several important ways,
Amish singing has also changed throughout the years. These changes have,
paradoxically, helped to retain the vitality, continuity, and flexibility of a
culture set apart. While the Amish are by no means dying out, singing
remains a central tool that regenerates their thriving and stable subculture.

This claim, which we will flesh out in coming chapters, leads us to several key questions for this study: In what ways does singing function to
develop a sense of being Amish? How does it build and sustain Amish
culture? What role does Amish singing play in worship and devotion,
communal memory, instruction, and enjoyment? How does it nurture and
socialize the singers, and how does it both maintain cultural consistency
while also anticipating and managing change? To these questions we now
turn.

CHAPTER 2

The Functions of Amish Singing

O Gott Schöpfer, Heiliger Geist,	*O God Creator, Holy Spirit,*
Zu Lob und Preis dir allermeist,	*To Your praise and glory most of all,*
Woll'n wir einträchtig singen,	*In unity we want to sing,*
Und nach den guten Gaben ringen.	*And strive after the good gifts.*

—*Ausbund,* Lied 50 (1564/1997).

I arrive at the farmstead one clear autumn morning and knock on the screen door. There is no answer although the inside door is open. Leaving the porch, I look for other signs of life in the garden and side yard. A man dressed in Amish blue, smudged with work dirt, emerges from the barn. "Good morning," I call out. He slows and greets me, with no apparent surprise at seeing me standing a few feet from his kitchen door.

Several weeks earlier, a colleague had suggested I meet her childcare provider, a young Amish woman named Elizabeth. While I was interviewing her, Elizabeth mentioned that her mother loves to sing and that I should talk to her. I set a date through Elizabeth and now am here to speak with her mother. So I tell the man that his daughter Elizabeth has invited me to talk with his wife, and he responds pleasantly, "Knock on the door. Anna's inside." I step up and knock again. A minute later, a woman appears at the door clutching the neckline of her forest green cotton dress in her left hand. "I was in the basement sorting potatoes and needed some pins to close up the bag. Come on in and give me a moment to re-pin myself," she explains with no hint of embarrassment. Her naturalness and kindness set me at ease.

When she returns, I offer her my gift of fruit. She leads me on a tour of her home. On the left is the living room where the men sit when it is her family's turn to host worship services, and on the right is the kitchen where the women sit. The minister stands in the doorway between the two groups, she tells me. The kitchen linoleum and wood are clean and buffed to a sheen. "My son made these cupboards as a gift. I stained them myself," she tells me. "Beyond that curtain is his room. He's the youngest and still lives at home." She points through a dark blue cotton sheet. Only one of her five children has married, although another son, who turned thirty, has moved to his own house up the road at the edge of their fields.

Anna shows me several of her hand-stitched quilts. "Four hundred and fifty dollars for this one, but some patterns take much more time," she tells me. When Elizabeth is home, she quilts too, but she far prefers to babysit for non-Amish families to earn her contribution to the family budget.

Anna invites me to sit at the kitchen table and serves us fruit and coffee. As we talk, she sings many songs for me, including her favorite, "Mockingbird Hill." She prefers that I do not record her singing but eagerly describes her experience of music as an Amish woman. "The slow songs come from the *Ausbund*," she tells me. "We sing them in worship, when we get together, and at home. The fast songs come from the *Liedersammlung* and some other hymnals and songbooks."

Darting under another sheet that separates the kitchen from a sitting room, she re-emerges with songbooks from long bus rides she and her family have taken to visit their relatives around the country. Anna tells me that they use these small 4-by–6-inch songbooks for pleasure singing. We peruse American folksong collections covered in various shades of green or blue cardstock. One index lists "This Land Is Your Land," gospel songs, and religious children's songs such as "Jesus Loves Me."

When I ask her what song she would sing to a child, Anna sings a fast melody to the four-hundred-year-old text of "Es sind zween Weg" (Musical Example 2.1). Singers use other melodies as recommended in side notes in the *Ausbund* and *Liedersammlung*. A few well-known melodies may be used for a dozen texts.

Anna sings the song lightly and joyously with a strong, pleasant, vibrato-free voice. As she finishes, I inquire, "What is the importance of singing to you? Why do the Amish sing?"

Anna shrugs and explains with a slight accent, "We enchoy it."[1]

Anna's answer is straightforward and simple. She answers with aplomb, as if the point should be obvious. Yet, Anna's response points to a

Musical Example 2.1. "Es sind zween Weg," Anna, Wayne County (1999).
Translation: *There are two ways in this our day,*
One narrow and the other broad.
Who now will go the other way
Will be despised by all abroad.

primary role of singing in Amish life: a pleasurable pastime that accompanies daily activities. Although few Amish people verbalize the effect that music has in building and sustaining their collective psyche, this examination will confirm that singing is a primary cultural practice that threads through Amish homes and community gatherings.

We should examine singing as an Amish pastime first and then move on to several other key roles of singing in Amish life.

Enjoyment

Anna is not alone in her articulation of enjoyment as a primary reason that Amish people sing. When surveyed, Amish adults usually speak of singing either for enjoyment or as an assumed part of everyday life. Of course, singing as a pleasurable activity occurs in most cultures. However, the priority that Amish people place on singing and the amount of time they report singing points to a particularly high level of enjoyment of the act. Over 90% of 56 Amish interviewees agree that singing is "important." Within that group, nearly 60% evaluate singing as "very important" in their lives (table 2.1). Many Amish people report that they sing as much as two hours a day while engaging in a variety of family chores and activities (table 2.2).[2]

Singing among the Amish is a sanctioned pleasure, a pastime approved by the church and occurring in nearly every setting of Amish life. When the Amish sing, they suspend time, freeing themselves from the routine of work.[3] Perhaps because of the lack of radios, computers, and televisions, singing gains primacy in Amish homes in a way that it may not in non-Amish homes. Like non-Amish families a generation ago who sang in the car with children in the backseat, Mom and Dad up front—a far cry from individual iPods or streaming cartoons and movies on factory-installed

Table 2.1. How important is singing in your family? (1999)

Perceived importance	Number responding	Percentage responding
Very important	33	58.9
Important	12	21.4
Somewhat	6	10.7
Not very	2	3.6
Not important	3	5.4
Total	56	100.0

Table 2.2 When do you sing? (1999)

Activity	Frequency			
	Often	Sometimes	Rarely	Never
Cooking	6	10	5	1
Housework	8	12	2	0
Gardening	1	10	10	3
Bathing a child	4	13	6	4
Buggy riding	5	9	6	2
Playtime	6	7	4	5
Other: sitting on the porch in the evening to relax, sewing, milking, bedtime, rocking, Sunday evening, mowing the lawn	3	1	0	0

video players—Amish families still enjoy singing in their buggies, passing the time and relishing the closeness and comfort of family.

Yet if singing functioned only as a vehicle for enjoyment among the Amish, it would hardly warrant book-length attention. Singing is clearly also about worship, instruction, nurturing, socialization, communal memory, and maintenance of culture.

Worship, Devotion, and Instruction

"We sing to praise God," one Amish person told me. "The *Ausbund* songs have special meaning," another said. Esther explains, "If you sing, it can minister to your heart." Perry recognizes, "Spiritual songs help to bring me closer to God." Another woman reports, "Singing keeps the thought life in check and gives you a spirit of gratefulness."[4]

How does music hallow and create the sacred space in Amish worship? The group gathers in a different Amish homestead every other week, opens with song, and transforms the mundane living area into a sanctuary. In Amish worship, singing is second only to preaching in importance. We will examine singing in worship contexts in more detail in part II, but it is critical to note here that Amish singing serves to uplift spirits, to express devotion, and to experience joy in faithfulness to God. One Amish man, speaking of the role of church hymns, clarifies, "A farmer would not think of sowing his seed without first getting the soil in shape"; by the same token, he says, singing the old hymns puts the Amish in a "prayerful, receptive mood" to the message of the succeeding sermon.[5]

The Amish believe that singing opens spiritual "ears" and shapes God-centered "hearts." It offers a body of concepts against which the members can examine themselves and sort their personal beliefs.[6] Music may open individuals to become aware of the true nature of their being, of an "other self" within the self, and link each in deeper ways to the surrounding community and God's creation.

The Amish choose songs that reinforce the beliefs of the group. The core values of respect for elders and other figures of authority, mutuality, equality, strong self-discipline, conformity to church discipline, separation from the world, *Gelassenheit* (yielding to God), and *Demutigkeit* (humility)—all of these evidence themselves in songs. Voicing the words deliberately at a slow speed, singers experience the song as a vehicle for instilling important messages.

Indeed, limits on the types of songs Amish people sing are often linked to this sense of singing as an expression of worship and devotion, and decisions about what songs are appropriate are made according to whether they are considered holy enough for Christians to sing. Anything modern is suspect. A survey of what the Amish call "fast" songs—usually gospel texts and tunes—suggests most were written prior to 1940. John Paul Raber, an Ohio Amish writer, agrees with the use of gospel tunes and texts only when they spread the teachings of Christianity. He cautions, however, that gospel songs "would not be so popular today" if they were truly preaching Christ, suggesting that popularity equates with worldliness. Raber further remarks that the founder of gospel music, "half God-fearing Thomas A. Dorsey and half good-time Georgia Tom,"[7] merges the "earnest fervor of spirituals with the Blues' swinging beat" into "rocking tunes," and because of this, discerning leaders felt forced to expel Dorsey from the church.[8] Therefore, while the Amish employ gospel tunes, they do so in a way that could never be accused of "swinging" the beat. Amish singing must always take a form that "glorifies God and does not spotlight humans."[9] Interestingly, Raber further disapproves of the use of choirs and quartets because, he says, they place undue attention on the singers.

George Brunk, a Mennonite bishop who advocates "divine simplicity" in songs, remarks that musical instruments are disallowed because the Protestant reformer Ulrich Zwingli rejected their use in church, along with other nonbiblical trappings such as candles, incense, crucifixes, and altars. According to Zwingli, "God ordained vocal music, the wicked added the instruments." Most Amish districts today do not allow instruments even at home. Ada Lendon, a formerly Amish woman, notes that her mother, who remains in the tradition, "liked to play the harmonica . . . I remember a boy in another district had an accordion. Boy! Could he play! He had to get rid of it to join the church."[10] When the Amish use only the specifically approved types of music, they participate in setting and maintaining boundaries for their communal life, boundaries that "liberate them from patterns of thought that might oppress them."[11]

When articles in Amish publications focus on singing, writers often affirm this role of music as a venue for worship and an encouragement to right living. The magazine *Family Life* devotes nine of thirty-six pages of one issue to a discussion of singing. In one article, "The Stranger and His Music," the anonymous writer proclaims, "The truth is music is a very powerful force. It can be a good influence, but it also has great potential for evil." The writer discriminates between the right and wrong kinds of music. An appropriate Amish song teaches sound doctrine, has a serious rather than sentimental or emotion-stirring content that is deeper than one can discover on first reading, and focuses on praising God, not bringing attention to the singer. The most valued songs are those composed by a "faithful, earnest martyr." The tune must be beautiful, restrained, modest, and without a heavy or foot-tapping beat, which would be "somewhat of a narcotic and too flashy." The melody should not be too easy, as short snatches of Scripture sung to snappy choruses are a worldly trend of which to be wary. And, of course, the preferred song texture is unison, "the most pristine sound on earth." The writer urges Amish adults to adhere to these guidelines when seeking appropriate songs.[12]

In the Amish teachers' publication *Blackboard Bulletin*, "Teacher Arlene" describes singing as a normative activity and asserts that all should participate for their own spiritual health and well-being. Amish interviewees may admit a feeling of inadequacy—"I don't have a good voice. You should hear Esther sing!"[13] Or an Amish teacher may judge her students' singing as average. One recommends that rather than listening to her class, I should go to a nearby school where the teacher "can really sing."[14] But "Teacher Arlene" expects that all sing without worry or shame:

> A normal child's attitude toward God begins in his own home. His parents are molding and shaping his attitude as a reflection of their own. This also is true of a child's attitude toward work and his own abilities and talents. If we excuse a child from doing something he doesn't want to do or thinks he can't do good enough, are we helping him? . . . I think there are many reasons why we should teach our children to sing . . . if we wish them to spend eternity in heaven, there will undoubtedly be singing there, and won't we be expected to help sing, regardless of how our voices are? . . . Let's not deny our children the opportunity of singing to allow them to develop the feeling of expressing their devotion and reverence in their hearts to God.[15]

By requiring participation, parents and teachers shape their children to the group's understanding of godliness. This attitude connects to another major function of Amish singing, nurture and socialization, which we examine next.

Nurture and Socialization

One of the primary roles of singing in Amish life is that of nurturing children to meet community standards, values, and expectations. Music builds solidarity and serves as a "marker of identity," whether or not the Amish consciously recognize this.[16] Singing unites the community as it does individual families. Through patterns of parenting, visiting, working, and worshiping, every care is taken to envelop children and youth into the extended family and larger community. Musical experiences are a part of each of these patterns.

In Amish communities, belief and way of life are inseparable.[17] While education in the dominant American culture promotes independence, self-advancement, and the acquisition of power, Amish education guides a child to live humbly and to be satisfied with simple living in resignation to the will of God.[18] The music of the dominant American culture—manifold, varied, simple, or complex—reflects a culture of difference, newness, and invention. The singing of the Amish, in contrast, embodies simplicity, conformity, and unity of a single line of melody, sung together as one voice, for the purpose of praising God. Singing affirms norms of behavior and, as ethnomusicologist John Blacking writes, "sentiments that [pre-] exist."[19] Singing reinforces the Amish way, specifically contentment in a life of work and family. Living spiritually and committing to the worship and praise of God with a pure, humble voice keeps an Amish person centered on faith. This stands in contrast to the ideas about singing that exist in the wider culture: that the best voice is a trained, self-conscious voice singing in a large public venue.

The parallel between music and language may be instructive as we investigate this question of nurture and socialization. Music is a language with multiple shadings of meaning, phrasing, syntax, enunciation, emphasis and understatement, and exposition of themes and ideas. People who both sing and speak any language might be accurately classified as bilingual. For spoken language, total immersion makes for mastery and native-speaking capacity. This may be the only way to incorporate nuances of pronunciation and meaning that are inaudible or untranslatable to non-native speakers. Similarly, Japanese violin master Shinichi Suzuki promotes the idea that very young children can learn to play music just as they learn their mother tongue—by living it. Suzuki instructs parents to play daily recordings of the music that the children are learning. The children hold their violins under their chins while building with blocks or doing other typical childhood activities. Music becomes the children's play and work and is integrated into their normal routine. In many Amish families, singing provides a comparable backdrop to daily chores and times of rest, in addition to the core of group singing events planned into the week. In this way, they surround their children with the songs—the language—of their faith community.

Very often, people can sing every word of a song without consciously considering the words, and if asked to write down the words without singing them, they would be hard pressed to do so. The words are wedded to the melody. Just so, Amish children may sing an *Ausbund* song without understanding the words at all, yet the music enters their body and mind, resonating in the nerves and synapses, moving the muscles, and creating and aligning the thought patterns, attitudes, and world view. Amish children develop feelings about and attachments to the songs on an emotional level. Later, through instruction in their homes, at school, in worship, or in a moment of self-realization, many children develop a comprehension of the meaning of the lyrics as historical and spiritual texts.

Communal Memory

Singing for the Amish is also one way to connect with with Anabaptist martyrs of the past and to challenge themselves to live a more rigorous and sacrificial faith. When an Amish woman sings martyr songs, she honors the martyrs while contemplating whether her own commitment is firm.

We will look at the *Ausbund*, the oldest Protestant hymnal in continuous use, in more detail in part III, but it is important to note here its crucial role in the formation and maintenance of communal memory.[20] The martyrs wrote these hymns while awaiting their deaths by hanging, drowning, or burning, singing to comfort and support each other. Amish worshippers sing one particular *Ausbund* hymn, the *Loblied*, also called the *Lobsang* and *Lobgesang*, as the second hymn in every service. This archetypal *Ausbund* hymn functions as a symbol of faith and heritage and as a way of memorializing the martyrs.

The memory of the martyrs, a formative element of Amish life, cannot be underestimated. Through singing ancient melodies and texts, Amish people regularly align themselves with the past. Their voices become vessels that carry the memory, identity, and devotion of their ancestors into the present.

Cultural Maintenance and Change

In the 1950s, sociologist Gertrude Enders Huntington's PhD advisor at Yale University told her to "hurry and study the Amish before they die out." So Huntington moved in with an Amish family and did just that.[21] That professor vastly underestimated Amish tenacity. More than sixty years later, the Amish have managed not only to survive but also to flourish. The Amish subculture functions as a nurturing ethnic group with a common language, common values, institutions, a taken-for-granted heritage, and transmitted qualities of patience and endurance.[22] For nearly 500 years, this group identity has fused due to experiences of outside aggression, deprivation, and discrimination, forging a durable cohesiveness.[23] Amish family routines, community customs, and religious practices aid the shared goal of upholding the group's cultural values.

Even careful observers may overlook the power of music in sustaining a culture. Few Amish articulate that their singing matters. They value specific texts but do not seem to recognize how, in the singing, the text, vocabulary, rhyme, melodic material, tune, rhythm, tempo, volume, human creativity, and cooperation coordinate to translate a society's commentary on life, from the silliest to the most profound, into song. Amish singing styles reflect their reliance on spiritual language and images in daily life, focus the mind and heart on the praise of God, and express expectations that the faithful will live apart, committed to social insularity. All of these aspects of singing contribute to the building and sustaining of their separatist culture.

Cautious as they are, the Amish oppose changes, and this resistance has become a cultural marker. Their musical life supports this resistance. Printing previously unwritten tunes in *Amische Lieder*, Amish writer Joseph Yoder advances, "Due to the Principle that 'change' is not desirable, the Amish people have continued to use this music for more than two and a half centuries."[24] Certainly, many cultures censor incoming cultural messages, but the Amish must relentlessly resist a large variety of music and a multitude of performance styles readily and steadily available to them in the dominant culture, such as in restaurants and other businesses where they work or shop. In religious music alone, there are dozens of styles, including Christian four-part hymns, gospel songs, Christian rock, punk, country, and European classical sacred music. The Amish reject much of this music as too worldly because it advances self-interest and, as such, is morally bankrupt.

In general terms, a group's art, whether it takes the form of cave drawings, cathedrals, or a cappella singing, functions to solidify community and reflects a deeper consciousness than an individual may be able to express through speech. Still, art does allow an individual to express the inner self, even expanding the limits of culture. Music, as a universal cultural attribute, "flowers" or is "suppressed" depending on the social environment. Blacking seeks to untangle the music-culture dialectic in order to develop a language for describing the underlying deep structure of the music within its cultural context. He chastises others for their lack of cultural understanding:

The purpose of the technique I advocated in *Venda Children's Songs* was not simply to describe the cultural background of the music as human behavior and *then* to analyze peculiarities of style in terms of rhythm, tonality, timbre, instrumentation, frequency of ascending or descending intervals, and other essentially musical terminology; but to describe *both* the music *and* its cultural background as dialectically interrelated parts of a total system. Because music is a humanly organized sound, there ought to be relationships between patterns of human organization and the patterns of the sound produced in the course of organized interaction.[25]

In music, one of the most highly structured of human cultural expressions, individuals must collaborate totally to make decisions about what, when, and how they will perform.[26] Each song and each singing event articulates an aspect of the culture's integrity. "No work of art (or single performance) can do justice to the whole complexity of reality. Every work of art is a simplification based on a convention," reiterates Blacking.[27] Then, in order to know a culture fully, one must participate ritually, including musically. A group's ritual sequence of baptism, animal sacrifice, watch night, or other activity accompanied by music counterbalances evil, disease, and death and generates energy and life.[28]

In his *Music, Culture and Experience,* John Blacking further proposes, "Music is non-referential and sensuous, and no claim can be made that it is directly political. But some music can become and be used as a symbol of group identity, regardless of its structure; and the structure of the music can be such that the conditions required for its performance generate feelings and relationships between people that enable positive thinking and action in fields that are not musical."[29]

Throughout the centuries of persecution and, perhaps more so, during the years of tolerance, the Amish have monitored the musical practices of their members, then prescribed and proscribed certain types of songs and singing. Like the ban on musical instruments, these choices have been made by the community to unite them in their resolutely simple way of life, which they believe to be redemptive. Other forms of singing, if tolerated, might lead their children to prefer the vain, pride-filled, and consumer- and achievement-oriented lifestyle of their non-Amish neighbors.

Singing among the Amish serves not just to sustain culture; it also reflects and helps to manage changes occurring within that culture. For example, even Old Order groups who affirm monophonic singing now find the part-singing of their New Order neighbors creeping into evening sings. Some Amish oppose part-singing, insisting that singing in unison confirms the emphasis on simplicity and a commitment to unity. Again, Blacking proposes that the establishment and maintenance of certain performance practices is a political act, "political in the sense that it may involve people in powerful shared experience within the framework of their cultural experience and thereby make them more aware of themselves and of their responsibility towards each other. Music is not then an escape from reality or a reinforcement of other political experience, it is itself an adventure into the reality of the sensuous and social capabilities of the species, and an experience of becoming in which individual consciousness is nurtured within the collective consciousness of the community."[30]

Blacking sees music as essential to humanness. He explains, "Music making is an inherited biological predisposition which is unique to the human species . . . [and] a symbolic expression of social and cultural organization, which reflects the values and the past and present ways of the human beings who create it."[31] Blacking's description accurately represents Amish public worship singing, where fifty to five hundred people sit together singing unison hymns of four to six stanzas with up to thirteen lines per stanza.[32] When Amish parents steep their children in the singing practices, they are, in fact, engaging in the process of instilling a cultural taste and a desire for Amish living.

However, some musicologists oversimplify causal links between music and culture. For example, Alan Lomax articulates a theory of *cantometrics*, an analytical system for understanding and classifying types of cultures. Lomax argues that, if a culture's song texture is monophonic—that is, one line of melody sung without harmony—it follows that the society is primitive and undeveloped.[33] Hence, native groups that sing only monophonically are more likely to use bone or stone than those that have developed harmony. Lomax claims that his system of analysis is "objective science [which] supplied us with certain incontrovertible proofs regarding the role of musical style as a reflection of certain fundamental truths."[34]

The Amish experience contradicts this value-laden presumption. They employ monophonic melodies but are not backward or uneducated (although they may be stereotyped as such). The fact that they teach children within the community and avoid many aspects of modernity is a conscious choice on moral grounds. Thus, the Amish singing style results from "intentional interaction by processes of decision-making by individuals," as

Blacking claims, rather than from a backward social reality.[35] The deliberate decision to bar the use of harmony from the worship setting or prohibit musical instruments reflects this process rather than signaling a primitive culture.

How much change may be tolerated? Again, Blacking predicts, "Musical change may precede and forecast other changes in society. It is like a stage of feeling towards a new order of things."[36] This might lead alarmists to warn that any tendency to allow "new" music, such as three- or four-part harmony, could lead to the extinction of the Amish culture. However, the Amish experiment with part-singing, and they sample other genres to see what effect, if any, these actions have on cultural assimilation. Indeed, if they should detect an erosion of their values, it is likely that they would reinstate previous limitations on the song choices.

Further, Blacking reports that musical change typically does not reflect a process of musical or technological development but usually occurs with the amalgamation of other groups. Even then, this is a process of choice.[37] Because the Amish do not proselytize, only rarely do they bring outside group members into the inner circle. The groups themselves decide what changes to make.

As we have seen, Amish singing is not static. Changes are occurring. Contact with the outside world has diluted and expanded Amish cultural practices. But, there are many aspects of singing that have remained inviolate. The place of singing in Amish life deserves critical review to determine its role as a vehicle for conveying cultural values and to calculate the relationship between musical changes and cultural changes. We will look more at the changes occurring within Amish singing in chapter 12, but for now, we turn our attention to one of the songs Anna sang for me—"Es sind zween Weg"—and the way in which it both signifies the boundaries that are so important to the maintenance of Amish culture and exemplifies the variety that exists within an Amish musical repertoire. We will also look at how this song typifies a common Amish singing style.

CHAPTER 3

Case Study: "Es sind zween Weg"

Es sind zween Weg in dieser Zeit,	*There are two ways in this our day,*
Der ein ist schmal, die andern weit	*One narrow and the other broad.*
Wer jetzt will gehn die schmale Bahn,	*Who now will go the other way*
Der wird veracht von jedermann.	*Will be despised by all abroad.*

—*Eine Unparteiische Liedersammlung* (1892/1999)

W e are human like you are. We make mistakes and we have to learn from them, just like you," the Amish man shares, as he speaks to the thirty-four students in my rural sociology class. "It's not any easier being Amish."

The class has just consumed a mammoth home-cooked feast in the whitewashed basement of an Amish home. One student eats eight pieces of homemade bread and asks to buy several loaves to take home. More times than I can keep track of, family members pass dishes of tossed salad, tender beef, succulent fried chicken, green beans with ham, noodles, mashed potatoes, gravy, and Dutch apple and cherry pies. The father jokes with the students and goads them to eat more. As everyone finishes their seconds (or thirds) of pie, our Amish speaker widens his table's conversation to include the whole class. Our hosts join in to answer the students' questions.

The discussion centers on the choices that the Amish make in order to remain faithful to their beliefs. "We adjust and adapt to the current times. We want our youth to remain within the community, so we are finding ways to be closer families again," the speaker continues, and our host agrees. The students want to know about *Rumspringa* and also about how Amish people in general decide which technologies to adopt or reject. The students' questions mirror the ones that they are asking for their own lives: how to choose one vocational path over another, one partner over another, one lifestyle over another. Both Amish and English youth frequently reach a crossroads at which they must make decisions, and both reflect on the question "Which way is the right way?"

We first look at the Amish hymn "Es sind zween Weg" as a lens through which to view this question of boundary development.[1] This deceptively simple concept of choosing between two ways, of course, proves more difficult to live than to sing. Nevertheless, "Es sind zween Weg" affirms an Amish belief in the opposing poles of acceptable, virtuous, and godly living versus an easy, worldly, fallen, disastrous, and cursed existence. Also, the hymn exemplifies both the consistency of musical and spiritual practice in Amish culture and the musical diversity of Amish singing life. We then consider the common style of singing among Amish communities as exemplified by this song.

Text of Divergent Ways

The text of "Es sind zween Weg" is rooted in both the Judeo-Christian and Greco-Roman traditions alluding to choosing between two ways— one narrow and one wide. This striking metaphor of human existence describes a lone individual standing at a crossroads, choosing between pleasure and fleeting satisfaction versus righteousness and integrity. Scriptures of the Judeo-Christian tradition frequently admonish believers to follow the "right" way, the way that leads to truth and life.[2]

The first biblical passage specifically referring to the wide and narrow ways dates to approximately 31 C.E.: "Enter ye in at the strait gate: for wide is the gate, and broad is the way, that leadeth to destruction, and many there be which go in thereat: Because strait is the gate, and narrow is the way, which leadeth unto life, and few there be that find it" (Matthew 7:13–14). Earlier Sophist writings, however, predate this reference by several centuries. In the fifth century B.C.E., Prodicus relates a parable about alternative paths to happiness—the short and easy and the long and arduous. Two specters appear as Vice and Virtue, and Hercules must choose. In the long term, choosing Virtue will bring him grace, love, and an abundant harvest.[3] In the fourth century B.C.E., Aristotle uses literary metaphor to describe his method of ethical training. His dialectic teaches that pairing virtues with vices aids in developing an understanding of both. Good may be comprehended as opposed to evil, bravery as to cow-ardice, righteousness as to vanity, and prudence as to wastefulness. These distinctions, he explains, are best related through storytelling, yet another art form.[4]

The interest in divergent ways continues in many philosophical and religious texts. Also, the visual art of German woodcuts of the twelfth century features the theme. The "Y," with one thick arm and one thin arm, symbolizes the wide and narrow roads.[5] By the fifteenth century, the Y-shaped symbol was familiar enough to be used as a crucifix and a scepter (figure 3.1).

For the Amish, choosing between the wide road, leading to fire, pun-ishment, and separation from God, or the narrow, reaching glory and re-ward, becomes a fundamental concept. Frequently interacting with others who claim to be Christians but do not follow the narrow path, the Amish, in their determination to be faithful, draw what Thomas Meyers calls "a clear cut boundary between the kingdom of the world and the kingdom of God. . . . The Amish sense of order, from their very beginnings, included a decisive need for boundaries."[6] By singing "Es sind zween Weg," the Amish delineate the boundary.

One Amish writer, Levi Miller (1996), recounts an allegory of the two ways in his pamphlet *A Pilgrim's Search*: "A broad road went to the left and a narrow path to the right. The King explained the road to the left would eventually lead back to the city of destruction, the world and on to eternal punishment."[7] This is the message of "Es sind zween Weg."

Figure 3.1 Y-Signum and Sceptre (German woodcuts, twelfth century). Geofroy Tory, *Champ Fleury* (Paris, 1529), quoted in Harms, *Homo Viator in Biviio*, 321. Ripa, *Iconologia* (Rome, 1603), 344.

Melodic Variations

Sung to many tunes, "Es sind zween Weg" appears in a variety of musical guises. Every Amish person easily sings several versions of the song. The first time she led a song in public, one Old Order Amish woman recalls singing "Es sind zween Weg" at a youth singing. "My father told me, 'When you can lead a song, you'll get a dollar,'" reminisces Anna (Musical Example 3.1).

Musical Example 3.1. "Es sind zween Weg," Anna, Wayne County (1999).

Another interviewee, Rachel, who downplays her singing ability, sings a melody beautifully with glides and slides. Her voice sounds ethereal as she vocalizes the old words (Musical Example 3.2). This melody utilizes only a narrow six-note range.

Musical Example 3.2. "Es sind zween Weg," Rachel, Holmes County (1999).
Source: Unidentified Amish woman, personal interview, 29 Oct. 1999.

Rachel sings two notes of equal length to most of the syllables, in contrast to a slow version of the song that a student recorded at the 2001 Wayne County Former Amish Reunion—hereafter referred to as FAR (see appendix I, Musical Example A1.1). At this semiannual gathering of former Amish, the women sing with feeling but leave out one line of

melody—the third—and sing the text of the third to the fourth line of
melody.[8]

Ethnomusicologist John Blacking observed this, too. He found that
"singers often omit 'lines' of standard songs" or may insert them in unexpected places.[9] Without apology, the leader at FAR provides a translation
of the first two lines and avoids comment on the third and fourth, despite
another woman mentioning quietly to my student that they omitted a line
due to a group memory lapse or nervousness at making a recording.

This version of "Es sind zween Weg" flows in a free rhythm, with no
set meter, sung slowly. The Amish also sing "Es sind zween Weg" to gospel melodies such as "I'm Building a Home."

Published Versions of "Es sind zween Weg"

The Amish maintain a considerable consistency despite their reliance on
oral transmission, a fact that can be seen by comparing sung versions to
several early published sources (see appendix I for comparisons). *Amische
Lieder*, published in 1942, was Joseph W. Yoder's effort to preserve the
texts and tunes from his Amish childhood. Yoder approached this project
by asking a group of experienced *Vorsingers* to sing hymns for him while he
transcribed them. In his collection, Yoder offers several different versions
of "Es sind zween Weg"[10] (see appendix I, Musical Example A1.2). Yoder
explains that he intends his publication to help families learn and use the
slow hymns for daily home worship. He prefaces his 1942 edition with
Amish directness: "Since the singers of the [Mifflin County, Pennsylva-
nia] Valley feel that they still have these hymns as near or nearer the old
ways of singing them, than any other community, it was only natural that
the writer should go back to the Valley to catalog these songs and hymns
in their early forms."[11]

Another version of "Es sind zween Weg," from the Library of Congress (1941), closely follows the Yoder (see appendix I, Musical Example
A1.2). The oral transmission of the song is remarkably consistent, and it
is not at all likely that the Amish singers have had access to the Library of
Congress version to guide their singing. Perhaps we can understand this
consistent transmission by comparing it to the tune of "Row, Row, Row
Your Boat," which hasn't changed in decades.

One more published example of "Es sind zween Weg" appears in a
1997 songbook entitled Ausbund *and* Liedersammlung *Songs,* which in-

cludes sixty-nine texts and melodies collected by Amishman Ben Troyer, Jr. Troyer uses a shape-note musical notation developed for Sunday school singing schools by William Little and William Smith in *The Easy Instructor* in 1801 and later employed in B. F. White and E. J. King's *The Sacred Harp*, published in 1844.[12] Troyer wrote all the notes in solid black shape notes: a triangle for "do," the first note of a major scale, which he calls a "firm, restful, conclusive" note; a square for "la," the second major scale note, which is "sad, sorrowful, wailing"; a circle for the third note, "sol," which is "bright and joyous"; and so forth.[13] Troyer gives neither rhythmic notation nor tempo markings, making it difficult for the uninitiated to know the intended rhythm. He explains, "For the sake of simplicity, no timing or duration of notes is observed in this book"[14] (see appendix I, Musical Example A1.2). The Troyer version of "Es sind zween Weg" is very close to the version sung for me at the reunion of formerly Amish people (table 3.1; see also appendix I, Musical Example A1.1).

Whether sung in a group with a strong *Vorsinger* or at home by oneself, whether sung in free rhythm, 3/4 time, or 4/4 time, whether sung to a gospel melody or a uniquely Amish one, each version of "Es sind zween Weg" enhances the words and promotes thinking about the serious choices the singers face. Singing "Es sind zween Weg" reinforces core values of humility and submission, as well as the necessity of walking a path of righteousness and wisdom.

Style of Singing

Several of the versions of "Es sind zween Weg" also underscore the singing style the Amish employ, which includes scooping and sliding to reach a note of a new syllable as the singers move between two syllables, the consistent use of anticipation, and melisma—the singing of a single syllable while moving to several different notes in succession (see especially Musical Example A1.1 for melisma and Musical Example 11.2 for anticipation).

Musicologist George Pullen Jackson, who studied Amish church chants and wrote his doctoral dissertation on Amish hymnology in 1954, reports hearing a tendency to melisma. He writes that the Amish sometimes even use ten to twenty notes per syllable, which he attributes to "vocal vagaries—tone waverings and rhythmic inconsistencies of the performances [that] become stylized and incorporated in performance prac-

Table 3.1 Comparison of the Former Amish Reunion and Troyer melodies

Text syllable	FAR melody	Troyer melody*
Es	E♭-C-B♭	E♭-C-B♭
sind	B♭	B♭
zween	**C-E♭	C-E♭-F-E♭
Weg	**E♭-B♭	E♭
in	E♭-F	E♭-F
die-	G-E♭	G-E♭
ser	**F-G-E♭	F-E♭
Zeit	E♭	E♭
Der	Missing	E♭-F
ein	"	G
is	"	A♭-F
schmal	"	G-F-E♭
der	"	E♭-F
an-	"	G-E♭
der	"	F-E♭-F
weit	"	F
Wer	Using line 2 lyrics for line 3 melody **D♭-F	E♭-F
jetzt	G	G
will	**B♭-F	A♭-F
gehn	G-F-E♭	G-F-E♭
die	E♭-F	E♭-F
schmal-	G-E♭	G-E♭
e	F-E♭-C	F-E♭-C
Bahn	C-E♭	C-E♭
Der	Using line 3 lyrics for line 4 melody F-G-F-E♭	F-G-F-E♭
werd	E♭-B♭	E♭-B♭
ver-	C-B♭	C-B♭
acht	C-E♭	C-E♭
von	E♭-F	E♭-F
je-	G-E♭	G-E♭
der-	**F-G-E♭	F-E♭
mann.	E♭	E♭

* No key given; same key used as for the FAR version.

** Differences between the FAR and the Troyer version.

tices."[15] Because the Amish transmit melodies orally, a strong singer can pull the group to his stylization of the rhythm, holding one note a little longer here, a little shorter there.

The final note is barely held a full beat and then is chopped off quickly. As in nearly all Amish singing, the *Vorsinger* sings the incipit, typically the melody for the first syllable of each line of text, then continues or pauses briefly, waiting for the others to join her. Whether in a schoolroom, at home, or in worship, the Amish are singing with people with whom they sing often. Like a well-rehearsed marching band, they match their stride to group norms in order to maintain uniformity.

Researchers throughout the twentieth century have noted other characteristics of Amish singing (see appendix III for a review of historical studies on Amish singing). In 1939, John Umble published an article in the *Journal of American Folklore* about Old Order Amish hymn tunes, proposing that "some of these are reminiscent of the Gregorian chant; others, if they are speeded up somewhat, bear a close resemblance to German folk tunes."[16] The similarities between Gregorian chant and Amish worship singing have been pointed out elsewhere, and some observers assume more similarity between the two forms than actually exists. Indeed, the similarities between the two are notable mostly to outsiders rather than to the singers themselves. At one meeting with Amish friends, I brought a recording of Gregorian chant and played it for them. Several of the Amish folks commented, "That's nice" or "That's interesting," but none of them ever alluded to the recording again or asked to hear other songs.

Several studies have discovered common attributes of Amish singing. In 1949, linguist J. William Frey described worship singing practices among the Amish, including the presence of a songleader (whom Frey called a *Vorsenger* or *Vorschtimmer*), the abrupt ending of the last note of each line, the lack of meter but presence of what Frey called a "clearly defined" thesis and arsis (or rise and fall of the melody), and embellishments in some of the voices.[17]

Charles Burkhart's 1952 master's thesis examined the music of Old Order Amish and Old Colony Mennonites; Burkhart makes observations similar to Frey's, noting especially the call-and-response between a *Vorsinger* and the group, monophonic singing in octaves, melismatic melodies in which each syllable of text is sung to three or more notes, and the extra slides and glides between pitches sung by a few individuals.[18] These observations are particularly true for the singing of *Ausbund* hymns.

In his 1957 article "The Hymns of the Amish: An Example of Marginal Survival," musicologist Bruno Nettl claims that Amish singing styles have changed little over the centuries and that isolated groups such as the Amish may be able to preserve a "lost" historical musical style. After theorizing as to the roots of the tunes of Amish worship songs, Nettl concludes that the melismas remained consistent even though the melodies have been "slowed and ornamented beyond recognition."[19]

Hedwig Durnbaugh's 1999 article "The Amish Singing Style: Theories of Its Origin and Description of Its Singularity" is one of the few recent assessments of Amish singing. Durnbaugh takes issue with Nettl's theory of "marginal survival" in the protected enclaves of the Amish. Durnbaugh finds it unlikely that the highly melismatic style of the Amish could have developed and survived in its current form. She agrees with Jackson that Amish singing has evolved from a syllabic style, with one note sung per syllable. By adding tones or tone waverings through the centuries, it finally reached the current melismatic style. Durnbaugh concludes that "step-wise weaving-around in the case of repeated tones and inserting passing notes in the case of intervals are natural ways of dealing with the challenge of either maintaining or arriving at the correct pitch."[20]

"Song Hunger"

For all their important contributions to an understanding of Amish singing styles, these researchers give scant attention to Amish singing outside of a worship setting. Nettl mentions that "little is known of the fast tunes" and then moves on to cover the slow hymns sung in worship.[21] Jackson dismisses nonworship songs because they are mainstream gospel hymns and "deserve therefore no more than a footnote listing here." Also, notable is the fact that Jackson claims that the incursions of tunes from Europe and folksongs such as "Froggy Went A-Courtin'" into Amish song life can be attributed to what he calls "song hunger." The Amish are "lyrically undernourished," Jackson proposes, and, as such, have needed to draw from outside of their tradition.[22]

Whether or not the Amish are "lyrically undernourished" is an issue that rests, of course, in the eye of the beholder. As we make our way through the song life of the Amish, however, I believe that most people will find a richly musical community quite different from the one Jackson perceived. As a partial remedy to the paucity of scholarship about non-worship singing among the Amish, we turn our attention in Part II to the singing that occurs in Amish homes in Amish schools and among Amish youth. We go first to the nursery songs that surround Amish infants when they enter the world and the songs that accompany an Amish childhood.

PART II

SINGING IN CHILDHOOD AND ADOLESCENCE

CHAPTER 4

Songs for Nurture
Lullabies and Children's Songs

Schlof, bubeli, schlof	*Sleep, baby, sleep*
Der Dadi hiet die Schof	*Grandpa tends the sheep*
Die Mammi hiet die dotti Kieh	*Grandma brings in the skinny cows*
Bawd in da dreck bis nuf in dee Gnee	*She wades in mud up to knees*
Un kommt net ham bis miah früh	*She don't come home until morning*
Schlof, bubeli, schlof.	*Sleep, baby, sleep.*

—Ada Lendon, personal interview, 26 July 1999

Miming the cradling and patting of an imaginary baby against his shoulder, an Amish grandfather recalls singing and soothing first one twin son then the other. "How many hours a day do we sing?" he chuckles as he repeats my question. "It depends on how many babies you have to rock!"

Now a bishop, Jacob Beachy reminisces about the many hours of singing his favorite song, "Es sind zween Weg," twenty-plus years ago to his own children. "And now we have four grandchildren next door," he offers meaningfully.[1] His wife tells me about the grandbaby born with a disease that doctors predicted would shorten her life to a few months. "We took turns rocking her day and night, and she was never alone. We had only a little time to love her," Erma recalls. "The doctors were surprised when she lived for eighteen months." We look deep into each other's eyes for a moment.

Later, Erma sings "Schlof, Bubeli, Schlof" for me and then hides a giggle behind her hand. She translates for me that Grandma is up to her knees in "mud," adding that this is a probable reference not simply to mud but to cow dung. We laugh, and I glimpse the young, carefree Amish girl still alive within this grandmother. She now sings for her grandchildren the same songs that, in all likelihood, her own grandparents sang to her.

As Erma's spouse Jacob suggests, singing to and with young children is a centerpiece of Amish parenting and grandparenting. Fifty-four out of fifty-six Amish interviewees in one survey state that they sing "daily" or "often" with young children. Yet, singing is only one strategy among many that Amish parents use. Before we look at the particular songs of an Amish childhood, we should examine Amish parenting more generally.

Amish Parenting

Amish parents lovingly and vigilantly nurture their children in Amish principles and values. Ministers at the Amish Ministers' Meeting of 1873 admonished parents, "Take very great care, you to whom the care of your children is so highly and preciously commended, that you bring them up from youth in the admonition of the Lord; for this is the greatest and most noble duty of the Christian."[2] The Amish take this charge seriously. With great consistency, Amish parents work to prepare their children for heaven. Amish parents, especially fathers, are seen as responsible for raising their children so that they will choose to be Amish. More specifically, they must account to God for how they turn out.[3] Rosemary O'Day writes, "The Reformation, by reducing the authority of the priest in society, simultaneously elevated the authority of lay heads of households" to require an accountability for the religious and moral education and conduct of both their wives and children.[4] Amish parents do not rely on any other institution, neither Amish private schools nor church fellowships, for their children's religious instruction. They believe it is their own responsibility. At school, children learn arithmetic and reading, not religion. In worship gatherings, children worship alongside their parents, not in a separate Sunday school.

The Amish perform neither christenings nor dedications of their infants, mainly to stay away from any appearance of infant baptism. Historically, adult baptism is the primary tenet of the Anabaptist tradition; their radical refusal to baptize their infants in spite of the state-church requirement elicited severe, brutal penalties. The community does welcome the newborn, however. Neighbors visit on Sundays or weekday evenings and bring treats for the mother. Men use the opportunity for fellowship. Friends assess whether additional help is needed and may send a teenage daughter to help with housework for a month or so. For twin births, the women of the district organize themselves to bring meals two times a week for two months, further evidence of a spirit of mutual aid.

Amish adults parent with kindness and firmness. They teach their children to fulfill their work responsibilities agreeably and without expecting thanks. Pleasure in accomplishing a task is seen as its own reward. "The dishes are clean and put away," a parent calmly observes, rather than offering a reward or other affirmation.[5]

Amish children ask, "Why?" as English children do. One Amish man emphasizes, "Give them the real answer. If it's important, tell them why."[6] When a mother writes to *Family Life* for advice about raising her "strong-willed child," an answer from "a mother of eight" recommends that the child "needs to feel secure before discipline is effective. . . . The source of a child's security is his parents and the more you hold them, cuddle them, nurse them as babies, and allow them to snuggle up to you night or day— the more secure they will feel."[7] Warmth, kindness, love, and attention open the child to accepting the authority and discipline of parents.

Adults appear reluctant to scold a child. "The scissors are sharp," an aunt cautions four-year-old Eli as she gently removes them from his hands. But from two years old until the teen years, parents begin to impose "restrictions and exacting discipline," according to John Hostetler, a scholar of Amish life, in order to teach the child to respect his elders and to recognize his "moral inadequacy" and the need to repent and commit to following Christ.[8]

Older children exert influence on younger children. Interdependence develops between siblings and cousins when young children accept help from those who are older and older children look out for the younger.[9] Older siblings "persuade and wheedle [younger siblings] into obedience," writes Hostetler.[10] Grandparents, aunts, uncles, and neighbors all contribute to the socialization of a child. However, the parents are the first and foremost influences. Amish children imitate their parents' example. Young children follow their fathers around the farm, patiently observing and helping as they are able. As the child grows, she is given specific chores, such as washing dishes, feeding chickens, or collecting eggs. One Amish woman remembers hanging song lyrics above the sink so her daughters would appreciate what they have: "Thanks God for dirty dishes. / They have a tale to tell. / While other folks are going hungry, / We're eating very well."[11] These daily influences have a predictable cumulative effect.

From the Cradle

As Jacob Beachy demonstrated, Amish infants are swaddled in their parents' and grandparents' singing from birth. But much more is at work in the image of Jacob rocking and singing to one of his grandchildren than simply a grandfather comforting a baby or soothing a tired child. "Early childhood music is not simply functional, that is, for entertainment or to quiet a child," writes ethnomusicologist Jeff Todd Titon. "It teaches the musical taste and orientation of a particular group. Lullabies not only lull but promise, praise and teach cultural values."[12] Music teaches a worldview, awakening the singer and listener to an expanded self- and community-awareness as they participate in the musical process. "We feel before we understand," notes ethnomusicologist and anthropologist John Blacking. "Affect motivates decision-making."[13] Singing helps the child feel the connection to and the protection of his parents emotionally before he comprehends these logically. How an Amish child feels about his family influences how he will feel about the community and helps him decide what it means to be Amish and whether he fits into, loves, and feels loyal to this group. The child learns the deeper structure of the community—the grounding principles, rules and expectations, values and norms—through song. First listening to and later singing these songs, the child internalizes the messages and, through each stage of life, sorts and sizes up the demands made upon her.

Historically, nursery songs stem from traditional dancing and singing games intended to ward off evil and invoke a healthy aura that promotes agricultural fecundity. Early examples are engaging, amusing, and highly symbolic. In one rhyming incantation, a woman sweeping finds a crooked sixpence, goes to town, and buys a pig. On the way home, the pig will not go over a stile, the ladder between fencerows. "And I shan't get home tonight," the woman complains.[14] The cumulative, series chant seeks to break a spell placed on an object by sneaking up on it through complicated repetitions. Framed like "The House That Jack Built," this Chaldean chant provides another example:

One only kid, one only kid, that father bought for two zuzims,
Then came the cat and ate the kid that father bought for two zuzims
Then came the dog that bit the cat that ate the kid that father bought for
    two zuzims.
Then came the staff that beat the dog . . .
Then came the fire that burned the staff . . .
Then came the water that quenched the fire . . .
Then came the ox that drank the water . . .
Then came the butcher who slew the ox . . .
Then came the angel of death that slew the butcher . . .
Then came the Holy One, blessed be He! And killed the angel of death.[15]

The cat eats the kid to set the process in motion. Jewish mystical (Haggadah) writers interpret the kid as the Hebrews; the father as Jehovah God; two zuzims, as Moses and Aaron; the dog, the Babylonians; the cat, the Assyrians; the staff, the Persians; the fire, Alexander the Great; the water, the Romans; the ox, the Saracens; the butcher, the Crusaders; and the angel of death, the Turks. The history of the Middle East is hidden in one child's story-game. Each aspect of the rhyme has a counterpart; for in magic, "every power is subservient to a stronger power."[16]

"Rockabye Baby" intimates that the consequences for those who aspire to rise too high will be dangerous, perhaps lethal: "Down will come baby, cradle and all." One version dating from 1670 cautions children that they are not too little to go to hell.[17] Whether parents aim to frighten children into submission or whether children take pleasure in being frightened, the themes of violence and mortality are often explored in nursery rhyme and song.

The early Anabaptists inhabited a world of infant mortality, folklore, ethnic infighting, and the like. Although Amish parents choose not to tell fairy tales, their telling of the stories of their martyred ancestors are gruesome and chilling enough. Moreover, stories of the Hebrews and the apostles in the Bible contain both moral teachings along with stories of cruel violence and brutality. In addition to these stories, Amish children hear and read real-life accounts of a practical nature that entertain and educate. Songs for Amish children often tell stories even as they create a space for attachment between parent and child and transmit cultural and religious values.

Several nursery songs recur when Amish parents list songs that express the values they seek to impart to their children. These are "Schlof, Bubeli, Schlof," "Raddy, Raddy, Gally," "Es sind zween Weg" (see chapter 3), the *Loblied* or *Lobsang* (see chapter 10), and "Bedenke Mensch, das Ende" (see chapters 1 and 13). The themes of each of these songs underscore the importance the Amish place on the extended family and on agriculture (whether a garden, animals, or crops), which remains an idealized Amish occupation. The repetition of songs becomes a powerful method of inculcating the idea of social harmony from an early age. Children daily hear soothing, gentle melodies and affirming, stirring words. "Schlof, Bubeli, Schlof" emphasizes the emotional well-being brought about by working together as a family while "Raddy, Raddy, Gally" evokes the sheer joy of parental love and the desire to hold children close, to have fun, and to socialize them into the Amish way. And "Es sind zween Weg" urges the Amish on their spiritual way.

The fact that Amish parents sing folksongs with messages about family life and love, like "Schlof, Bubeli, Schlof," might be surprising to some who expect that the Amish only seek to religiously indoctrinate their children. Understanding that Amish parents and grandparents enjoy their children and grandchildren and act warmly toward them humanizes the Amish. They are people who care for and love their children. Discovering the variety of family singing habits and the meaning behind them may moderate prejudices about the Amish as dour, emotionless people.

We now look at "Schlof, Bubeli, Schlof" and "Raddy, Raddy, Gally" in more detail before moving on to several other beloved children's songs.

"Schlof, Bubeli, Schlof"

When interviewed about songs they sing to their babies, many Amish adults first name "Schlof, Bubeli, Schlof" ("Sleep, Baby, Sleep"). Or if I mention the title, women and men alike greet this most familiar song title with huge smiles and laughs of delight. They explain that *Bubeli* is a term of endearment for babies, whereas for older children it might be used in a teasing or exasperated tone: "Stop being a *Bubeli* (baby)."

Emily Gerstner-Hirzel documents many versions of this song in German language folksong, from "Ruh, Kindlein, ruh / der Wächter tutet: uh" to "Schloop Kinneke schloop / in Marias Schöötje" and "Schlaf Babele schlaf / und scheiss mer net aufs Wendele." The earliest known version from Bremen was published in 1767, well after the Amish had already departed for America. The most similar texts related to agriculture come from Basel, Lower Franconia (Germany), and Lancaster, Pennsylvania[18] (table 4.1). The Swiss still sing this song, reports Wayne Weaver, a physician who grew up Amish and who visited Switzerland in the 1990s.

In *Singing Mennonite*, Doreen Klassen catalogues Mennonite songs brought to Canada from Russia. She documents five "Sleep, Baby, Sleep" versions. Comparing these to Amish versions, Klassen notes many variants in the lyrics of her five versions but relates that the "melodic differences were minimal."[19] It seems likely that this song, sung as early as 1767, went to Russia with Mennonite emigrants and to the American colonies with Mennonites and Amish people. Texts and tunes have changed somewhat, but they are essentially the same song with a similar message and simple folk-style melody.

Klassen translates one version, "Sleep, baby, sleep, your father herds the sheep / Your mother shakes a little tree / There falls down a little dream / Sleep, baby, sleep." Another version takes on an edge: "Sleep, baby, sleep / Outside stand the sheep / A black one and a white one / And if the baby won't sleep / Then the black one will come and bite it."[20]

Table 4.1 Historical "Schlof" songs, Gerstner-Hirzel (1984)

Date	Song title/lyric	Location
1767	"Slaap Kindken slaap / dien Vader is een Aap / dine Moder is een Etterlin / slaap du verwesseld Horenkind"	Bremen
1853	"Schlaf Büble schlaf"	Tirol
1894	"Schlof Chindli schlof / di Muetter hüetet d Schof"	Basel
n.d.	"Schlaf Kindlein schlaf / dein Vater hüt die Schaf / dei Mutter hüt die dürra Küh / kommt nich heim bis morgen früh."	Lower Franconia
1915	"Schlof Bubbeli schlof / der Dawdy hüt die Schof / die Mommy hüt die rote Küh / un steht im Dreck bis an die Knie."	Lancaster, Pennsylvania
1918	"Schlof schlof schlof / der Tate wet fohren in Dorf / wet er brejngen an Epele / wet sain gesund die Kepele."	Munich (Yiddish version)

The Canadian version resembles the tune of a Pennsylvania version Ruth Hausman describes in *Sing and Dance with the Pennsylvania Dutch*, published in 1953. Although the Canadian version is in the key of F in 2/4 time and the Pennsylvania version, in the key of G, swings in 6/8 time (Musical Example 4.1), the rise and fall of the melody is the same.

Musical Example 4.1. "Schlof, Bubeli, Schlof," Lancaster, Pennsylvania, version.
Source: Hausman, *Sing and Dance*, 66–67.

Hausman reports that Amish settlers brought this song from Germany to Pennsylvania in the 1780s. Through the centuries, men and women have frequently moved between settlements to marry a spouse or to find affordable farmland or increased seclusion. Hence, no district can become musically isolated. One man of true pioneering spirit explains that when he married, he moved to Canada and then twice more, to Delaware and upstate New York, to inaugurate new communities. Amish interviewees acknowledge that, when newcomers join an established community, they generally match their singing style, pitch, and tempo to their adopted group's singing. But undoubtedly, there is some measure of mutual sharing.

A young Amish woman working in a community business in Holmes County sings a local Ohio version for me. Barbara agrees to have her song recorded, which is unusual given that the Amish consider recordings, as well as photography, to be vain. Her melody differs from Hausman's, and she adds a two-measure phrase (Musical Example 4.2). A comparison of the melodies in the Canada, Ohio, and Pennsylvania versions of "Schlof, Bubeli, Schlof" shows more similarity at the beginning of the first phrase than at the end (tables 4.2 and 4.3).

Musical Example 4.2. "Shlof, Bubeli, Shlof," Barbara, Walnut Creek, Ohio (1999).
Source: Barbara. Interview by author, Walnut Creek, Ohio, 26 Jan. 1999.
Translated by an Amish interviewee.

Translation: *Sleep, baby, sleep, Grandpa tends the sheep. Grandma brings in the skinny cows, / She wades in mud up to knees. She don't come home until tomorrow morning. Sleep, baby, sleep.* (Klassen's version is sung at the speed of quarter note = 76 beats per minute in 2/4 meter. This is faster than the one Barbara sings at mostly dotted quarter note = 57. Barbara begins in 2/4 [at quarter = 70] and switches into 6/8 meter when she gets into full swing. Barbara uses a three-note, do-re-mi scale while Klassen employs a five-note, do-re-mi-fa-sol scale with an additional sol below do, strikingly different. The Hausman version has the same scale pattern as the Klassen version. Klassen's and Hausman's are both written at a higher pitch than Barbara's [a third and a triton, respectively]. [See appendix I, table A1.1.])

Table 4.2 Comparison of three melodies (Canada, Pennsylvania, and Ohio)
transposed into C

Version	Text and melody			
	Sleep, little one	Sleep. Your	Father watches the	Sheep. Your
Canada	E DD	C A	EE DD	C EE
Pennsylvania	E DED	C A	EE DED	C A
Ohio	E DD	C D	EE DD	C D
	Mother, the little	Calves will tend, thru	Mea-dows green their	
Canada	FF DD	G EE	FF DD	
Pennsylvania	FFF DDD	GGG EE	FF DD	
Ohio	EE DD	EE D	EEE DD	
	Way will wend,	Sleep, little one,	sleep	
Canada	G E	E DD	C	
Pennsylvania	GG E	E DED	C	
Ohio	EEE DD EE D	EDD	C	

Table 4.3 Comparison of intervals in "Schlof, Bubeli, Schlof"

Interval	Canadian Russian Mennonite (Klassen)	Walnut Creek, Ohio (Barbara)	Lancaster County (Hausman)
Minor 2nd	2	—	1
Major 2nd	6	All	12
Minor 3rd	4	—	4
Major 3rd	1	—	—
Perfect 4th	3	—	4
Major 6th	1	—	1
Minor 7th	—	—	1

When Barbara writes the words for "Schlof," she uses an alternative spelling, "Shlof." This happens quite frequently, as Pennsylvania Dutch is a spoken, not a written, language and has no standardized spelling

In "Schlof, Bubeli, Schlof," the agrarian theme of "Grandpa tends the sheep / Grandma brings in the skinny cows" emphasizes the security and regularity of mother, father, and grandparents tending the farm animals in the nearby corral. Everyone helps. All are productive and effective workers. Song texts like these, with their themes of rural life, love of the land, and faithful work, reveal sets of expectations that Amish parents hold for their children.

"Raddy, Raddy, Gally"

If "Schlof, Bubeli, Schlof" encourages cooperation and diligence, "Raddy, Raddy, Gally" signals the joy of being alive. Parents intone the sing-song chant "Raddy, Raddy, Gally" while bouncing a toddler on a knee. Ada Lendon laughs as she sings "Raddy." Then she keeps on chuckling as she sounds out the words so that I can write down the lyrics (Musical Example 4.3).

Harvey Troyer offers a similar, rhythmic chant in an abbreviated version: "Ride-y, ride-y horsie / A mile'n'a half an hour. / Drive over a ditch / And dump off." The rhythm, somewhat uneven despite the racing pace, follows speech patterns and resonates with the cadence of clopping horse hooves, a common sound in the Amish child's life. The song is an unpitched chant, emphasizing rhythm rather than employing a melody.

In both versions, the singers choose an uncharacteristically quick speed,

Musical Example 4.3. "Raddy, Raddy, Gally," Ada Lendon (1999).
Source: Ada Lendon. Interview by author, Wooster, Ohio, 26 July 1999.
Translation by another Amish interviewee.
Translation: *Ride-y, ride-y horsey / Half an hour a mile /*
Tomorrow we have to thrash oats / For the horsey to eat food /
Then we go over the bridge / And the bridge breaks down.

giving the impression that thrilling the child is the song's major purpose.[21]
While singing "Raddy, Raddy, Gally," the adult jostles the child on his or
her knee. In Ada Lendon's version, the bridge breaks and the buggy overturns. In Harvey Troyer's version, an inexpert driver and too much speed
cause the accident. Evidently, some parents sing the third verse with the
addition of "Down into a ditch!" and dump the child onto the ground.

In the traditional English song "This Is the Way the Farmers Ride,"
the parent bounces the child a little higher and faster on each verse. My
own non-Amish family sang this song and added a fourth verse, based on
the radio and television show "The Lone Ranger": "This is the way the
cowboys ride, Hi ho, Silver, AWAY!" sings the adult, rearing the knees
up like a bronco and ending with the child upside down (see appendix I,
Musical Example A1.4). As each verse details the different riding paces of
ladies, gentlemen, and farmers, "This Is the Way the Farmers Ride" echoes
gender and class status distinctions. The parallel Amish rhyme, "Raddy,"
just describes agricultural life, with an emphasis on working in the fields.

Other Children's Songs

Amish parents I interviewed often had to think for a moment when asked
about singing and parenting. Hesitatingly, they would answer by listing
songs they sing often. They describe singing English nursery songs such
as "Ten Little Indians" and "Here We Go Round the Mulberry Bush" as
well as Christian children's songs such as "Fishers of Men" (see appendix
I, Musical Example A1.5) and "Jesus Loves Me" ("Jesus liebt mich") to
their children in both German and English. Amish adults relate that they

also sing "fast" songs such as "At Calvary" and "Amazing Grace"—hymns they learned in school, at Sunday night singings, and various family and community gatherings.

Amish parents enjoy singing gospel songs translated into German, including "What a Friend We Have in Jesus," "Jesus Loves the Little Children" ("Jesus liebt de kleine Kinder"), "Will the Circle Be Unbroken," "Sweet Hour of Prayer," "He Leadeth Me," and "I'm Building a Home." In the late nineteenth century, the Amish began to collect hymns into songbooks such as the *Unparteiische Liedersammlung*. The Amish do not sing these particularly fast, but they are distinguished as "fast" relative to the slowly sung *Ausbund* songs. Like other traditional Amish music, these songs are usually sung monophonically—that is, as one melodic line without accompaniment. But, some groups may harmonize them in three or four parts.

Parents recall singing comical songs, too: "Oh Fritzly hole mit some Cider ruh" ("Bring Me Down Some Cider"), "Ald Butter Fas" ("Old Butter Churn"), and "Meine Mutter mit de shlop Cop on" ("My Mother with Her Farm Bonnet"). Considering what songs she sang to her children, one Amish mother replies, "Anything that taught them to be humble." One Amish man tells me, "I'm seventy-eight and don't sing as much as before. I used to sing while rocking children to sleep a half hour to an hour a day. I sang mostly church hymns."[22]

When asked about the importance of singing in her family of origin, one Amish woman explains, "Singing is good for the heart and it is a privilege to be able to sing. We loved to sit on the porch in the evening and sing as a family." Another woman replies, "Singing transmits our values. It cheers up my kids and makes them ready to go to work." "A lot of songs have a message in them like a sermon," verifies another.[23] The replies quickly become familiar as, one after another, Amish adults answer consistently.

Changes in Singing with Children

Yet, like other aspects of Amish life, songs of nurture sung in Amish homes are changing. Some Amish interviewees wonder aloud whether singing will retain its centrality to the worship and social life of their communities. Indeed, it appears that Amish parents are singing slightly less often with their children than their parents did with them. More than 53 percent of 56 Amish interviewees evaluate singing as of the same or greater importance in their current family situation as it was during their child-hoods, with 12.5 percent assessing singing as more important in their cur-rent family. And 46.4 percent express that singing was more important in the family in which they grew up. Will this change have an effect on the cohesiveness of the Amish family or the vitality of music among the Amish? Perhaps. But even children whose families do not greatly value or engage in singing have plenty of opportunities to participate in singing through church, youth singings, and school singing. Perhaps the locus of singing is moving out of the home as the community gathers to reinforce family teachings.

The Amish school has become one of the major venues in which Amish singing practices are transmitted, and it is the venue to which we now turn. Visiting numerous Amish schoolhouses, I discovered that each con-tained a unique musical atmosphere, depending on the personalities of the teachers, students, and parents. Each school I visited confirmed my sus-picion that singing among the Amish—even among the youngest in their communities—remains a robust, lively, and daily expression of their cul-ture and faith.

CHAPTER 5

Songs for Instruction
Singing at School

Unveränderlich bist du,	*Unchangeable Thou art,*
Nimmer still und doch in ruh	*Never still and yet at rest,*
Jahreszeiten du regierst,	*Thou rulest the seasons of the year,*
Und sie ordentlich enführst.	*And bringest each one in at the proper time.*

—*Unparthenisches Gesang-Buch* (1997)

On a cold spring morning near West Salem, Ohio, I pick my way through the mud outside an Amish schoolhouse where I have come to hear the children sing. Despite walking gingerly, I manage to sink up to my ankle in cold water and mud, and I am relieved when I reach the porch. The young teacher, a man of eighteen or twenty, is just rounding the corner of the building, and he invites me inside. He has no beard, but a curly chestnut fringe of hair protrudes from under his hat.

Inside, the children, called scholars, are sweeping. They have moved desks aside and are using brooms ineffectually to push dirt and scraps of paper around the floor. It's a good effort although there is no real gain that I can see. In Pennsylvania Dutch, the teacher directs the scholars to replace the desks, and the workers immediately comply. He speaks very softly. A few others surround the potbelly stove. It is about 37 degrees outside and only 10 degrees warmer inside. I keep my coat on but the children have shed theirs, apparently possessing more faith in the heating capacity of that old stove than I have.

From their dress and hairstyles, the children appear to belong to the Swartzentruber Amish, the most traditional Amish group. Swartzentruber families have chosen not to have running water or modern bathroom facilities in their homes, nor do they use gas appliances, such as gas stoves, as many less strict Amish would. I remember that two Swartzentruber children I met at an Old Order Amish school south of Wooster started school at age seven having barely spoken any English at home.

The teacher, who introduces himself as Joseph, rings a handbell, and five of the girls slip on their high-topped, lace-up black shoes and run to the outhouse. When they return, they kick them off—either to limit the mud in the classroom or because their feet are warmer without the wet shoes. Several of the girls have holes in their black socks. One has no heel in one sock; another, no soles at all. The second pulls the sock over her toes to cover her feet, exhibiting no embarrassment. Some of the children have torn clothes, including flapping pockets, while others sport well-mended ones.

Ready to get the day going, the teacher glances out the window and notices two boys struggling down the road hauling a huge, round water cooler between them. One of them also carries a medium-sized, rectangular cooler, probably containing his lunch. Neither boy is more than ten years old. "We'll wait for them," Joseph informs me. I note with a bit of surprise that he does not run out to help but allows them autonomy.

One of the girls eyes me and softly asks the teacher in Pennsylvania Dutch, "Why is she here?" "To listen to singing," he answers. "Does she understand us?" One girl replies in English, "If we talk in English." She has no obvious accent.

When the boys get to the door, the teacher takes the cooler from them and hoists it onto a shelf in the back of the classroom. He places it next to a five-pound wedge of Colby-Jack cheese loosely covered with plastic wrap. A large knife protrudes from this help-yourself community property.

With spring coming late this year, it is cold season, and half of the children are coughing. One girl pulls a handkerchief as large as a dishtowel from inside her desk, starts with her nose, and mops her whole face dramatically. I stifle a laugh. The desks are loaded, overflowing with school supplies. Joseph leaves to bring in another armload of wood. In his brief absence, I try to strike up a conversation with several girls with no success.

The class usually has fifteen scholars, Joseph tells me. Today there are thirteen—nine girls and five boys. Black scarves cover the girls' hair, and I see snoods just visible at the napes of their necks. All but one wear blue jackets over blue dresses with matching aprons; the odd girl has a deep purple dress-apron combination. Three of the girls are older, looking to be in sixth or seventh grade. The five boys all have bowl haircuts and wear blue shirts and black vests. One girl sits by herself on the left side of the room, the rest in the rows on the right. Three pairs of children double up, two to a desk, for the opening singing time.

At the teacher's direction, the scholars start to sing automatically and unselfconsciously. Joseph turns his attention to some writing in front of him and does not participate in the singing. The thirteen children raise the roof, singing with spirited voices. The singing is lively and in tune, what most listeners would pronounce "ethereal," and the most enthusiastic of my experience in Amish schools. Yet, the children's faces appear expressionless. One girl of six or seven, who sits directly in front of the teacher, sings an octave above the rest consistently. No one comments, nor does she seem to know she is doing anything differently. I think back to the words of one of my music history professors, who once explained that organum (a medieval chant melody with an additional harmonic part) probably originated "accidentally" when singers sang at an octave, fifth, fourth, or even third or sixth below or above the rest of a group.[1] The effect, appreciated and copied, developed into modern harmonizing.

The *Vorsinger* for the day chooses a song, then sings a first syllable incipit for each line of every verse, and the rest of the singers come in on the second syllable. The children sing "Gott ist die Liebe" from *Ein Unparteiische Liedersammlung*.

After finishing the requisite three songs, heads swivel to look at me— whether for approval or to see what I will do next. I smile and *sotto voce* mouth, "*Danke schön*." As the children slip back to their own seats, I wave to Joseph, slip out, and slog back through the spongy schoolyard to my car.

History of Amish Schooling

One of the key factors supporting the Amish community's continuation has been the rise of the Amish school like the one I visited near West Salem on that chilly spring day. In the middle of the twentieth century, John Hostetler and Gertrude Enders Huntington write that American public schools began to be "controlled by the middle class and reflected their values regardless of the cultural composition of the students attending that school." In growing numbers, the Amish decided to build and run private schools that they themselves could supervise. Within the decade 1945– 1955, the Amish opened forty-four new schools across the United States;

in the decade of 1995–2006, 590 additional Amish schools opened, for a total of 1,436 schools.[2]

The curriculum of a school has a powerful role in shaping a child's awareness of herself and her world. Educator Henry Giroux explains that "curriculum can be viewed as a cultural script that introduces students to particular forms of reason, that structure specific stories and ways of life ... [They] explore a language of possibility that is capable of thinking risky thoughts, that engage a project of hope."[3] Amish parents and teachers developed a curriculum based on the homogeneity of their beliefs that emphasized a practical learning, leading to "a disciplined life on earth, concern for others and eternity in heaven."[4] The Amish gear their curriculum, including singing, to teaching their children what they need to know to be committed members of their community.

The return to the one-room school has been a hopeful, life-giving move, which has led to the increased viability of the Amish way of life. Don Kraybill and Carl Bowman write that, as "vital agents in [the Amish] protest against progress," these schools "insulate youth from Enlightenment notions of moral relativity, evolution, critical thinking and individualism ... [and] provide a cradle of ethnic friendships and minimize ties with outside peers."[5] Yet, the Amish school movement has served not as a nostalgic return to the past but as a reclaiming of their autonomy and a re-imagining of the steps needed to ensure a strong, positive future. The school atmosphere models the order and mutual concern that are the backbone of the Amish tradition. A common language, dress, and an emphasis on work, obedience to elders, and accountability to neighbors all conspire in this process of socialization to raise a child "so carefully within the Amish family and community that he never feels secure outside it."[6]

Amish parents take an active role in school policy and involve themselves in the day-to-day operation of the school. Amish teachers do not teach religion; nevertheless, "They practice their faith all day long, in Arithmetic, by accuracy (no cheating); in English, by learning to say what we mean; in History, by humanity (kindness, mercy); in Health, by teaching cleanliness and thriftiness; in Geography, by learning to make an honest living from the soil; in Music, by singing praises to God; on the school ground, by teaching honesty, respect, sincerity, humbleness, yes, the Golden Rule."[7]

As a vital part of the Amish school project, each day Amish schoolchildren review and strengthen their Amish identity by singing a narrow body of songs: songs about loving God, facing the imminence of death, relying on family ties, caring for the land, living a godly life, and even playing baseball underline the values of simplicity, conformity, and yielding to God. They also bolster the vision of the ideal Amish personality. Being work oriented, kind, gentle, obedient, and discerning about what is worthwhile in life all stand out as key characteristics. A significant part of the school day is English and German singing.

Singing practices vary by school, based on the capabilities and personalities of teachers, students, and parents and on the traits of particular districts or varieties of Amish. We will look at the specific repertoire of songs in Amish schools in more detail in the following chapter, but for now we outline some of the contours of Amish school singing and look at the musical assumptions and qualities that are shared across Amish schools.

Shared Singing Practices

Children in most Amish schools, usually with the participation of their teacher or teachers, sing for the first twenty to thirty minutes of the day. Scholars employ the traditional Amish singing practices, which include singing without instrumental accompaniment and in unison, with an occasional round.

Girls and boys in Amish schools take turns leading as *Vorsinger*, just as in other mixed gatherings besides worship. Sitting at her desk, the leader chooses a song and establishes the pitch and tempo simply by beginning to sing, with no other cues to the rest of the students. The leader continues to lead by singing the first syllable of each verse, rather than each line of text, as in *Ausbund* singing. The rest of the children join in on the second syllable, some jumping right in, others seemingly less prepared to join or thinking more slowly. Only rarely does the leader sing louder than the rest to guide the group. On occasion, the teacher has new songs she or he wants to teach the children. Even when the teacher herself leads the singing, she blends in, and no single voice dominates. Overall, the singing tends to be rather desultory, although enthusiastic singing by the teacher or a particular *Vorsinger* encourages the whole group and increases the singing energy. At one school I visited, the *Vorsinger* led with such exuberance that the girl sitting in front of him, who I guessed was his sister, turned around and gave him a pointed stare.

The tempo of each song tends to fit the customary speed of that particular group. In some schools, the children sing all the songs faster, in others they sing lugubriously. In my experience, the tempo does not correlate to the more or less traditional nature of the group. Texts tend to be sung slowly to emphasize the words and allow time to consider them. The slides and glides between notes give what some have called a "Buck Owens twang."[8] Many children use a pitch decoration called *anticipation*, in which the singer slurs the note on a word of text from one pitch to the pitch of the next word of text. The anticipations in this song are the second note in the first full measure (on the syllable "morning") as well as the second, sixth, and seventh full measures (Musical Example 5.1). Without any direction to do so, the children stagger their breathing so that there are no gaps between phrases. They use no vibrato, and the final note of a phrase is held for one beat rather than sustained.

Musical Example 5.1: "In Life's Morning," Traditional.

One clear difference between worship singing and school singing is that many of the school songs employ a metered rhythm unlike the distinctive *Ausbund* "slow songs" that characterize Amish worship singing. They also use set meters, usually 4/4 or common time, that is, four beats to a measure, and the quarter note gets one beat. The schoolchildren do not strictly adhere to the meter, however; for example, some notes are not held to the full note length, making the measure only three or three-and-a-half beats long in a 4/4 time signature. Since school songs are borrowed from other sources, such as evangelical church hymnals, school songs have only one or two notes per syllable of text while the *Ausbund* songs consist of three to eight notes per syllable.

The "fast songs," which scholars still sing at a moderate speed, derive from a mixed American musical songbook of gospel songs, folksongs, spirituals, and older country music.[9] In one school, as I page through a copy of a songbook of mimeographed lyrics titled *Our School Favorites*, I find someone had penciled "Clementine" next to the song title, "In Life's Morning," a song about working in the service of God and others. This is the melody the children use. They make use of anticipations as they sing (Musical Example 5.1).

The text of "In Life's Morning" is a distilled version of Amish values, which emphasize working with cheer and unflappable, unfailing kindness, and ends with the line "We are happy anywhere" in the final verse.

In Amish schools, the tunes used, even for the same text, vary. Some are very traditional, just like church chants. Others are folksongs. For a gospel song, "At Calvary," a song about finding salvation in the cross of Christ, the children use a standard gospel tune but make all the notes the same length instead of using the syncopated rhythm non-Amish employ. Similarly, in the Sharp Run Christmas program, when the parents and children sing "Stille Nacht," they use three even quarter notes in a waltz-like rhythm rather than the typical dotted quarter and eighth note.

As noted earlier, singing practices and traits vary between schools. The singing at the Zion Christian School, for example, where the children are both Amish and Mennonite, provides an interesting contrast. Scholars themselves lead the songs, as is typical in other schools, and the songs are all faith based. But in this seventh- to twelfth-grade class of about thirty, only a half-dozen of whom are Amish, students all sing in four-part harmony, which creates a beautiful, rich, full, unaccompanied "Mennonite" sound. They stand in the front of the room, some leaning against the blackboard, roughly in three rows. The Amish children join in, but they appear slightly abashed, looking down and standing a bit apart. The miens and affects of these Amish children, attending a school with non-Amish children, emphasizes the important role that the Amish schools play in nurturing feelings of belonging and security in children from kindergarten into their teen years.

But whether Amish children attend school with children from Mennonite families or only with their Amish peers, school singing reflects the same messages as home and worship singing. The simple melodies, the strong, plain words, the moderate tempos, and the joint effort converge to make a cooperative song event. Through song, Amish scholars console, encourage, instruct, and merge themselves with their community and with their ancestors. During childhood, scholars prepare themselves for their adult role as parents who will nurture their own children to be faithful followers of God.

We look now at some of the specific songs sung within Amish schools, beginning with one of the songs frequently sung in Amish schoolhouses.

CHAPTER 6

Case Study: School Repertoire

In der stillen Einsamkeit	*In silent solitude*
Findest Du mein Lob bereit.	*You will find me praising you.*
Großer Gott, erhöre mich,	*Great God, please listen to me*
Denn mein Herze suchet Dich.	*Because my heart searches for you.*

—*Eine Unparteiische Liedersammlung* (1892/1999)

The *Vorsinger* for the day announces the page number. "One hundred and seventy-six," says Junior, a gawky fifth-grader with a mop of thick blondish hair. The children race to be the first to find the page in the *Liedersammlung*. Every school I visit owns this hymnbook with spiritual hymns and psalms first collected by Old Order Mennonites in Pennsylvania in 1804.[1] The *Liedersammlung* includes hymns from the *Ausbund* and songs from other eighteenth-century collections. The smooth, black, hardback volumes seem well used, rubbed shiny, but are in unexpectedly good condition. The children have learned to take care of the classroom supplies.

I turn to the page and immediately recognize the song. Written by Joachim Neander in the 1600s, "In der stillen Einsamkeit" is a meditation hymn. God has ordered the universe, and humans respond with awe, praise, devotion, and thanks. I've heard this song in four other schools, but to date, each group has used a different melody. I'm eager to find out how this version sounds.

I glance around the school. The children sit in pairs on the desk benches, youngers with olders, modeling appropriate behavior and helping with finding songs in the books. The teacher is relaxed, sitting with her book open. Her fast-paced work will begin shortly. Through the window, I see the requisite tetherball hanging from and bouncing in the breeze against its silver pole and the softball backstop a little farther away. All in good time, the school day will unfold with lessons, recess, children's chatter, teacher's questions, spelling tests, and handwriting assignments. But after Junior sings the single note of the first syllable, and the others join in on the second, the children dedicate their day to God (Musical Example 6.1).[2]

Musical Example 6.1. "In der stillen Einsamkeit," Holmes County Amish school (2007).
Source: Ada Lendon. Interview by author, Wooster, Ohio, 26 July 1999.
Translation by another Amish interviewee.
Translation: (*verse 2*) *You do not change.*
Ever silent and still with your hand
You rule the seasons
And order them.
(*verse 8*) *It doesn't matter if outside it freezes,*
My heart is warm as I think of you.
Praise and thanks are here,
My dear Lord, in solitude.

I think back to the versions of the song I've heard in other Amish schools. One group sings one verse and then intersperses a chorus of "You'll Never Miss Your Mother 'Til She's Gone" in an upbeat, spirited rendition without any sentimentality. Another class adds the phrase "at the cross" in English as a tag to each line (see appendix I, Musical Example A1.6). Another sings two verses of the hymn and then sings a canon with the hymn text "Father, We Adore Thee" as a chorus; the group continues to alternate two verses of "In der stillen" with one chorus of "Father, We Adore Thee." The group stays fairly well on pitch until the final chorus, when the pitch unintentionally rises by a half-step.

Although the tunes and method of singing them vary across schools, "In der stillen Einsamkeit" remains a favorite among Amish schoolchildren.

This seventeenth-century song, which speaks of the order of creation and of human devotion in the face of God's grandeur, is a good starting point for our survey of favorite songs among the young scholars in Amish schoolhouses in Ohio.

A List of Favorites

Amish children freely choose more religious than nonreligious songs to sing at the opening of their school day. Based on listening to singing sessions in more than twenty Amish schools, I formulated a list of their favorite songs (see appendix II, table A2.1). As even a cursory glance at the list makes apparent, funny and frivolous texts, such as "Der Hund" (about a dog that bays at the wrong tree) and the "Bronco Song" (about a bronco that throws all riders into the briars), are few and far between. Scholars tend to pick "In der stillen Einsamkeit," "Es sind zween Weg," "Wir singen dir, Immanuel"—with extra "Hallelujahs!"—and other songs from the *Liedersammlung*. They also select gospel and youth favorites such as "My Life Is a Canvas," "I Was Made in His Likeness (and Born to Serve the Lord)," "I Know Who Hung the Stars," "Boys and Girls for Jesus," and an Amish favorite, sung at every nonworship Amish gathering, "Gott ist die Liebe."

Writing about Amish schools, Sara Fisher and Rachel Stahl report that two mornings a week, Amish scholars sing German songs; three mornings, English songs.[3] I found much more variety than their study seems to indicate. Some schools sing in English except for special favorites, such as "Gott ist die Liebe." In one Old Order school, the teachers explain that they always sing in German; another school only sings in German on Fridays. In ten of the schools, scholars sing at least one German song each day that I visit. However, in all the schools I visited, the selection of English titles is more diverse and more plentiful, perhaps because students focus on learning English while in school. We will look at some of the German songs in Amish schoolhouse repertoires first and then some of the English ones.

German songs. When scholars in Amish schools sing in German, they sing a limited number of texts. As mentioned earlier, five of the school groups I visited sing "In der stillen Einsamkeit," all sung to different tunes; three sing "Es sind zween Weg," using two different tunes. When choosing songs with which their classmates are less familiar, *Vorsingers* risk poor success in their attempts to pull the group along. More or less latitude in song choice depends on the school, but all of the schools I visited at least own copies of the *Liedersammlung*, which contains only song texts in German.

In one Old Order Amish school I visited, after the scholars stand to recite the Lord's Prayer in German, an eighth-grade girl chooses and leads the first song, a hymn based on Matthew 4:17. She loudly and confidently declares: "Create Your Blessedness" (see appendix I, Musical Example A1.7). In this school, the children only sing German songs. With no pause, another designated child announces the number of the next song and leads with timid voice, "O Vater! Kindlich beten wir."

Singing songs in the German language connects Amish children to their history and tradition in a profound manner. Simply using the language of the martyrs of their faith gives unspoken but weighty credence to the past. Outsiders to the Amish tradition may find it fascinating that songs like "In der stillen Einsamkeit" and "Bedenke Mensch, Das Ende," written over three centuries ago and sung in German, can elicit such an emotional resonance with contemporary Amish schoolchildren. Given the frequency with which children themselves choose these particular songs, however, it is evident that the songs of the past are alive and well among the youngest members of Amish communities.

English songs. The English songs sung in Amish schoolhouses are a combination of religious and nonreligious texts and tunes. Many are sung in a lively manner and may include motions. In one school, where English is the regular fare, two children choose songs: "The Wonder of Love" and "If You're Happy and You Know It." The children clap and stomp with real enthusiasm. Another child selects the action song "Peter, James, and John," a Bible story song and an apparent class favorite. The children turn in my direction as they "cast their nets on the OTHER side of the boat." Completely involved, their faces beam. One *Vorsinger* chooses a Bible story song about the Good Samaritan, "From Jerusalem to Jericho."

In another school, the children use American Sign Language for two verses and two choruses of "Jesus Loves Me." For the name "Jesus," the children motion to each palm of their hands with the middle finger of the other, alluding to the nail piercings of the crucifixion. Engrossed, they obviously enjoy singing songs with actions. At this school, the children lead two songs, and the teacher leads one, "I learned about Jesus in Grandma's

Rocking Chair," a southern gospel song written by Joel Hemphill and recorded by his family in 1975. Like most groups, these children sing the
choruses more confidently and enthusiastically than the verses of each
song. One seven-year-old squeezes her lips between her fingers to feel her
lips move as she sings. Another six- or seven-year old locks gazes with me,
and when I finally look away, she slaps her forehead. I smile in amusement.
The sound is full and rich. One boy sings an octave below the rest of the
children, still on pitch with the others.

Next, they sing a gospel song at half tempo, sliding between the notes
and anticipating the note of the next syllable of text. An immigrant from
Ireland and a minister of the Methodist Episcopal Church, William
Hunter, born in 1811, wrote the text to the second hymn, "I Feel Like
Travelin' On" ("My heavenly home is bright and fair, I feel like travelin'
on. / Nor pain, nor death can enter there, I feel like travelin' on"). The
tune is marked traditional, which means it probably has a Scotch-Irish
origin. The scholars do not sing cohesively but are dragging each other
along, working out the tempo between them, with no designated director.
Sitting near me sprawled in his chair, one larger boy, off in his own little
world, is not singing at all.

Their version of "This Land Is Your Land," the old folk favorite, reverberates with their joy at being faithful stewards of God's earth. Once
again, the scholars add anticipations to the melody.

At one school, I am surprised to hear scholars sing a selection made
famous by American pop singer—actress Doris Day in 1949, "There's a
Bluebird on Your Windowsill." One teacher reports that they sing a *Liedersammlung* text to this tune. She tried several texts but could not remember the one whose lyrics fit.

Whether they are singing in German or English, young scholars in
Amish schoolhouses learn the songs that shape their understandings of the
world and that mold their behavior. Amish writer John Coblentz states,
"We can learn to know what is in a [hu]man's heart by listening to his
song."[4] The Amish believe that what a child sings comes from her heart,
but what she sings also *forms* her heart. "Too much listening is not healthy
for that inner melody,"[5] writes Coblentz.

In my visits to Amish schools, it becomes apparent that some Amish
children enjoy singing and that others do not. The Amish expect that all
will conform and carry their own weight just as they must "bear each other's burdens." They believe singing will be required in heaven, so singing

is seen as preparation for an Amish child's final destination. Children must be allowed the opportunity, as one Amish woman writes, "to develop the feeling of expressing their devotion and reverence in their hearts to God."[6]

As Amish children become teenagers, their participation in youth sings will further mold that devotion and reverence. It is to these musical, religious, and social events for Amish adolescents that we now turn.

CHAPTER 7

Songs of Identity
Youth Sings

Once I was lost in sin, I had no peace within,
To save my weary soul I knew not how;
But Jesus came to me, and by His grace I'm free,
Now it's diff'rent, O so diff'rent now.
It's diff'rent now, Since Jesus save my soul,
It's diff'rent now, Since by His blood I'm whole;
Old Satan had to flee when Jesus rescued me,
Now it's diff'rent, O so diff'rent now.
—David Beatty (1958)

Dusk is deepening as I wind my way south toward Berlin, Ohio. Since the county roads dogleg, uphill and down, and since many buggies are heading north and south, I creep along. Presumably the buggies are carrying Amish youth to singings like the one to which I'm headed. One buggy I pass has no slow-moving vehicle markings at all, another has an orange triangle, and a third sports red and yellow flashers. Each belongs to a different community whose *Ordnung* requires greater or lesser simplicity. Some see lights and markings as ostentatious. Three buggies are heading up the hill a half-mile from my destination. I relax as I follow behind them. I can't pass until we top the rise.

As I turn into the blacktop drive, I observe several young men unhitching the buggies they have aligned with dozens of others in a field enclosed by a clean white fence. The hosts are scurrying back and forth between the house and the workshop with large covered pots holding food for our dinner. I park on the blacktop driveway near two other cars and enter the workshop to see men and boys congregating at the far end. Women, girls, small children, and babies are gathered at the end closer to me, next to a stove, shelves, and tables loaded with pots and pans. I am surprised to see every age represented, from five-month-old babies to eighty-year-old elders. This fact quickly overturns one of my assumptions about "youth" singings. They are run by youth but attended by many family members and friends of the host family. I count about ninety people in all, and everyone seems to be engaged in conversation.

At about 6:15 our host, Myron, greets the group and announces that we will open by singing "How Great Thou Art." He leads by singing the first word in a strong, clear baritone, and we all join in four-part harmony and sing two verses and two choruses of the hymn from memory. A full sound warms the workshop. When the hymn ends, heads bow in unison, and Myron offers a prayer of thanks for the meal that is to follow.

A line forms at the long table as age groups take turns serving themselves—youth first, followed by the men. To my surprise, the mothers with children wait patiently, along with some of the older women, until almost everyone else has gone through the line. No child complains or whines, and no one is in a hurry.

Tonight's fare is "breakfast dinner," several women warn me. I hear a hint of apology in their voices, but I assure them that breakfast has always been my favorite meal and that I already have my eye on the fluffy, soft-ball-sized cinnamon rolls. The menu for the evening also includes French toast, fresh fruit slush, hash-brown casserole, and cream-filled applesauce cake. Several women invite me to serve myself, and we eat together and talk. One asks me if I am a teacher and what I teach. I mention a summer course I teach on African music in Ghana, and the young mother takes me by surprise when she says her brother is teaching near Cape Coast. Another woman volunteers that she has two daughters teaching at a Mennonite school in Mexico.

Other youth groups arrive discreetly after the dinner hour. The gathering swells with two vanloads of youth. Often, local Amish youth groups—in this case, the youth of three districts—sing and interact together. The host family invites nearby family members and a few neighbors to participate.

Several young children help the men place German hymnbooks, *Eine Unparteiische Liedersammlung*, at intervals on the narrow benches, one book for every two or three people. Teenage girls file in from washing dishes

in the basement kitchen of the house and sit in five rows near the middle
of the room, facing the boys and men. The boys fill their rows, facing the
girls and women. This is a reversal; during worship, the oldest sit in the
middle rows and the youngest at the edges. The older women and men sit
on benches and chairs at the back of their respective sides. An equal number of males and females are present. The chatty and lively fellowship that
occurred over the meal ends, and the room becomes silent as we wait for
the first *Vorsinger* to open the singing.

This evening is for the teens. They take charge and show their capabilities by managing the dinner and leading the singing. A boy calls out the
first hymn number. With barely a pause, he sings the first syllable. Most
have not had time to find the page. The voices stagger in a bit unevenly.
Soon, the four-part harmony is rich and full, 130 voices strong.

The singing has begun.

An Overview of Youth Sings

Amish adults are thrilled that their youth exhibit an increasing interest
in singing. Many teenage boys work to learn the *Ausbund* songs so that
someday they may be asked to lead singing in worship. With no radio or
television, families still engage in singing. But the youth truly cannot wait
to attend Sunday night sings.

Youth singings serve as vehicles for teaching the important tenets of
Amish life and for enfolding adolescents into the life of the community.
In corporate singing in this setting, which is less formal than a worship
service, Amish teenagers also rehearse their identities, practice Christian
devotion, bond with peers, and prepare for full-fledged Amish adulthood.

The youth of a district may gather on Sunday if the home where their
district has held church that morning has youth-group-aged adolescents.
In this area, three districts collaborate so that the youth can meet people
from outside their district. Some youth find they have invitations to as
many as five youth singings on the same night. Youth-group leaders inform
each other of their scheduled singings. A group with around fifty members typically hosts over a hundred guests.

The host family serves a substantial meal, often of beef or grilled chicken
and potatoes. One family reported that they cut apart an oil drum and fit-
ted it with large racks for cooking quantities of meats. Additional treats
may include mashed potatoes, salads, homemade desserts, or store-bought

ice cream. Occasionally, simpler fare such as sandwiches and noodles is on the menu. Large jugs of water are a necessity.

Families often buy and bring their own hymnals to sings. When the singing begins after supper, the group sings for the first half-hour in German, followed by the devotional, led by the father of the hosting family or a minister or bishop, if the father prefers. The group then sings in English for forty-five minutes before spending more time visiting.

Even though the church tunes are, in the words of one Amish person, "pretty much the same" for Old Order and New Order Amish groups, the music for pleasure-singing varies.[1] The Old Order Amish still sing in unison. "We want to concentrate on the *words*," one Old Order person says with emphasis. "The New Order sings two or three tones at the same time. We don't. We sing all together. We don't believe in drawing honor to ourselves. It's what we're singing, not the tune."[2]

Part-singing has become the norm for Holmes County New Order youth sings such as the one at Myron's house that I attended. One woman declares, "Young people are good at learning new songs and have the time and opportunity to practice them." "They sing so fast!" remarks another woman of New Order youth singings. The adults often feel that they need to supervise the type of songs the youth sing. "They can't just sing anything they want," a woman explains. Her husband agrees. "We worried that if they sang four-part, fast songs that the youth wouldn't want to sing the slow songs," he tells me. "It has turned out that this interest in singing has spurred a revitalized interest in the slow songs, and youth men from sixteen up come to men's singings to learn the slow songs better. The young ones are leading in worship now." The joy in his voice is unmistakable.

Singings and Courtship

Youth sings are a longstanding arrangement by which the community assembles young people from sixteen to marriageable age. An Old Order Amish woman reports that some older Amish young people choose to stop going to youth singings if they feel they are past marriageable age and no longer fit with the group. As I've noted, however, some "youth" sings include a much broader range of ages. New Order Amish districts in Ohio have instituted Wednesday evening Bible studies for youth, which further knit the youth together and serve to help young men and women get to know each other. This practice lets the Sunday-evening singing provide another community-building event for all ages. These community fellowships designed for youth are undeniably successful in keeping Amish youth in the community.

Because dating is for finding an appropriate mate, not for flirting or having fun, the purpose of youth singings has changed. Amish youth used to date at sixteen or seventeen. Now, they are at least eighteen or have joined the church. "Marriage isn't for children, after all," one man explains. "It's a big commitment for a lifetime." Among the Old Order Amish, another man admits, the youth were "unruly and out of control." Some areas settled by the Amish have reputations for having wilder youth. The New Order Amish have shaped the youth groups and sings so as to maximize community building. In the old days, some Amish adults reported that youth stayed after the adults left to play games, dancing games like "Skip to My Lou" and kissing games. Now for the New Order, the youth singing serves as a spiritual gathering, a time to sing songs that emphasize their faith commitment. Amish youth do find marriage mates at sings and other youth gatherings.

In earlier times, couples were secretive about their courtship, but this is not as true today. If a young man wants to get to know a young woman, he asks at mid-week Bible study if he can come to visit her on Sunday. If she answers in the affirmative, he spends the afternoon after church with her, dines with her family, takes her to the evening singing, and brings her home. The Amish discourage long courtships because this puts too much pressure on the couple, leading to unwelcome and unwholesome behavior.

Toward the end of the New Order singing that I attend, I ask one woman if the boys and girls talk to each other during sings, as I have not seen them interact all evening. "Not during singings," she tells me. "They have opportunities at Bible study or at other youth events."

Let's return to that sing and explore it as a musical experience. The songs that the group sings, while notated in the hymnals that many Christian groups use, become the group's own as the singers alter and shape them. The group employs the distinctive Amish singing styles when they perform.

At a New Order Singing

We finish the first German song and then sit for a three- or four-minute silence. I'm not certain whether we are to be thinking about the words of the song or simply waiting for the next *Vorsinger* to choose a song. A girl eventually calls out the second number, and she begins right away. From then on, the leadership alternates between teen boy and girl.

I can hear the men's voices boom with a full sound as they sing facing in our direction. Because I am in the second to last row of women, I find it difficult to hear the women's voices in balance. The overall sound is pleasant, and it is obvious that everyone knows what they are doing.

We devote the first half-hour to German singing from the *Liedersammlung* and end with "Nun danket alle Gott," a famous hymn written in the mid-1600s by a Lutheran minister in Saxony for a celebration to mark the end of a famine and plague brought on by the Thirty Years' War. In 1840, Felix Mendelssohn harmonized the hymn. A female *Vorsinger* leads.

After the last German selection, a thirty-five-year-old man stands up at one side of the gathering between the men and women. He gives a short, earnest sermon—in English, because of my presence and that of another visitor. It focuses on choices and the importance of choosing to forgive. He holds up the families of the Amish girls killed in the Nickel Mines schoolhouse shooting in Pennsylvania in October 2006 as role models of people who are practicing forgiveness. After reading a short section from Romans and leading the group in prayer, he seats himself.

Several people leave for a quick break, presumably to the house to use the bathrooms. None of the women I am sitting with leave, so neither do I. A few minutes later I am handed a black, clothbound English hymnal called *Inspirational Songs.*[3] A teenaged boy calls out a number so softly none of us in the back rows can hear. We wait for others to telegraph us the page number as the singing restarts.

Many of the English songs we sing employ a call-and-response pattern between the male and female voices. This group disregards most accidental markings—sharps, flats, and naturals that raise or lower a note—and instead sings diatonically or within the key. In early musical notation, musicians limited *musica ficta*, or notes outside the key, to a flatted seventh note for the purpose of softening a dissonance. In the Late Middle Ages accidentals were added as the aesthetic sense changed. Musical Example 7.1a shows the way the hymn is written in *Inspirational Songs*; example 7.1b depicts how the group actually sings the line.

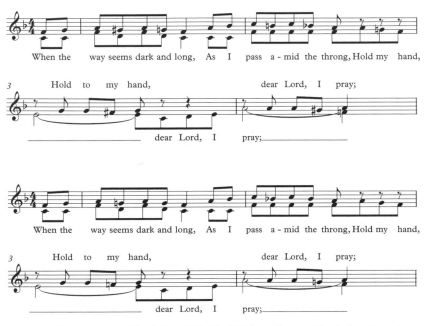

Musical Example 7.1. "Lord, Lead Me On," Holmes County Youth Sing (2010). *Top*, written, *bottom*, sung.

Later in the song, the altos, as they lead, again ignore a written A-flat and sing A-natural, another example of the group's use of a note within the key rather than an accidental. In two other songs, "What a Day That Will Be" and "Just a Closer Walk with Thee," the gathering also ignores the accidentals. I continue to notice accidentals frequently being deleted from songs throughout the singing. While the Amish in this area resist using the accidentals that non-Amish would use, no one I ask can explain why. Perhaps, these accidentals are too modern for their taste.

At times the group also alters the rhythm of the printed music. When singing "Hide Me, Rock of Ages," for example, the singers lengthen an initial dotted quarter note (in 4/4 time) by at least a sixteenth beat as though they are crying to God for help. The succeeding eighth note, then, comes in late. The rest of the piece follows in strict rhythm. In these deletions of accidentals and changes of rhythm, the group makes the songs their own and enlivens them with particularities that depart from the printed tune.

The group does sing all verses of the songs that are printed. Rather incredibly, the group sings at the pitch written in the English hymnals without resorting to pitch pipes. Who in the room has perfect pitch? No one seems to know. Strong, full singing continues throughout the evening, but my voice is wearing out.

By around 8:00 PM, the younger children have reached their limit, tired of sitting and singing. They walk back and forth to an orange ten-gallon cooler against the wall on the women's side, taking turns getting water using one of five plastic cups. Still, they are respectful and quiet and do not interrupt the gathering. They play with toys and read small books their mothers offer them. Older children lead the smaller ones out to the house when they need a comfort break.

At 9:00, the singing ends. Suddenly, I hear no more hymn numbers, and the girls turn to their neighbors and begin talking. As if on cue, everyone talks at full voice. When I leave at 9:45, the youth, boys with boys and girls with girls, continue their lively conversations. They will stay another fifteen minutes to half-hour. "We don't like to mix spiritual and social events. This is spiritual. They'll have time for social exchanges at youth group," an Amish friend explains later.

Wednesday Evening Bible Study

My Amish friend has been referring to the Bible studies or "youth groups" that take place on Wednesday evenings, organized for the New Order youth in Ohio to provide another opportunity for young people to bond through singing. For the typical youth group leadership, one boy serves as leader, another as treasurer, and a girl as songleader. The group appoints the leader to set plans for its activities. The treasurer holds the youth funds collected during each meeting. These are not dues as such because each person gives as they can and want. Monthly, the treasurer transfers the accumulated money to a minister. The money pays for group expenses, such as volleyball nets or donations to needy people, both Amish and English. For a special treat, like a pizza delivery from East of Chicago or Pizza Hut, everyone puts in the same amount, around five dollars. The song leader helps organize meals for the Wednesday meeting. She plans the menu and contacts everyone to let each know what part of the meal to bring.

The Wednesday evening meeting for New Order youth focuses on Bible study and song. The song leader chooses another girl to lead the songs each week. That girl chooses three German songs and may ask others to lead. Each week the youth memorize a verse from the Bible passage they are studying. The last person chosen the previous week chooses two boys and two girls to recite the memory verse aloud. Youth take turns reading one verse each from a chapter of the Bible. If there are more people than verses in the evening's chapter, they will start over and read until everyone has read a verse. The minister stands up and explains the meaning of the verses. Anyone can join the discussion, but some chapters engender livelier conversation. Working their way through every book of the New Testament, one group I visited had just finished Philippians.

After studying the Bible, the youth collect a freewill offering. They sing four more songs in English. One group sings from the *Church and Sunday School Song Book*. *Vorsingers* pick their songs by the message of the text and the sound of the melody. They like to practice in advance of the singing to get to know where the problems in rhythm or melody will be. They might choose to pitch the song lower or higher when they determine how it will work with the group's vocal range. Many familiar tunes are borrowed to use with texts from the *Liedersammlung*. One youth group sang "Ach bleib bei uns, Herr Jesu Christ" to the tune usually sung to Isaac Watts's hymn text "When I Survey the Wondrous Cross."

Occasionally, Amish youth meet on Friday evenings for entertainment or a service activity. This might consist of playing volleyball, singing for shut-ins, going to a rescue mission or nursing home, planting and maintaining a potato patch to earn extra funds for mission projects, or even hosting a murder mystery dinner.

Youth in the Amish culture receive regular attention and guidance from their parents and grandparents. The New Order youth singing and youth group meeting serve as vehicles for teaching the important tenets of Amish life. Yes, humility is valued. But more importantly, a change of heart and a willingness to allow Jesus to "pilot" their lives have become central. In the last hymn of one evening sing, the New Order group sings "It's Different Now." They recognize, "Once I was lost in sin, I had no peace within . . . It's different now, since by His blood I'm whole; Old Satan had to flee when Jesus rescued me." The singers stop on "me" and hold for three beats, then end with "Now it's diff'rent, O so diff'rent now."

Many of the songs that the New Order youth choose at the singing emphasize a faithful "walk," a life guided by the principles of God's Word and in relationship with Jesus. The youth sing to rehearse their identity as participants in a separatist religious group. They sing to connect themselves to their peers.

PART III

❦ Singing for Worship ❧

CR CHAPTER 8 DO

Songs of Memory

The *Ausbund*

O Herre Gott in deinem Thron,	*O Lord God on Thy throne,*
Du hast zum ersten geben	*Thou hast first of all given*
Dein'm Volk viel Recht und Sitten schon,	*Thy people many decrees and traditions*
Darnach sie sollen leben.	*By which they are supposed to live.*
Aber dasselbig alles hast	*But all of this Thou hast summed up*
In zwen verwiest durch Jesum Christ:	*Into two parts through Jesus Christ:*
Die Lieb das ist,	*The love that is*
Gegen dir und dem Nächsten.	*Toward Thee and the neighbor.*

—German verse from *Ausbund* (Amish Book Committee); translation from
Our Heritage, Hope and Faith (2000)

A half-hour before the 8:30 AM worship service, I meet the bishop
and his wife at their home. Since the Ohio summer temperature
has already climbed to the mid-80s, we decide to ride in my car
rather than walk the half-mile uphill. I park under a ten-year-old Norway
maple tree, hoping to garner a bit of shade from the blazing August sun.
The men are gathering in the barn; the women, in an attached concrete-
block workshop. The host family has scrubbed both buildings spit-shine
clean in preparation for the services.

The bishop's wife walks with me into the workshop. She places a brief
kiss on the lips of all of the women except me and another visitor, and the
women converse among themselves. After a few minutes, Erma consults a
large clock on the wall. "I wonder if Sarah and Ida are coming," she muses,
adding as an aside to me, "They're sisters who come together." These are
the oldest women of the district, and usually they would lead the line of

women who arrange themselves in the seats on one side of the room. Erma decides to go ahead, and she motions me to walk with the older women to take one of seven cushioned seats. I demur, but she insists. Within the hour, I realize the gift of the seat back, and three hours later, I will be deliriously happy to have soft padding.

The rest of the women line up and walk to backless wooden benches. In parallel lines, the men and boys organize themselves and process to the benches on the opposite side. The leaders, all males, and the rest of the older men sit facing each other in the two rows nearest the oldest women with the first row of women looking at the backs of one row of men. When he is reading Scripture or preaching, the minister will stand between the two facing rows of men (figure 8.1). The youngest boys sit in the back row and throughout the service duck out to check on the horses stabled in the barn. In all, forty-five people have assembled.

The service begins with a song, Scripture reading, and then two more songs. During the second of the three songs, the ministers and bishop leave and form the *Abrot*, or ministers' council. In this session, they give instruction to two teenagers seeking to join the church and plan who will lead in worship and who will preach each of the two sermons. When they return, one of the ministers preaches a half-hour sermon, after which the congregation rises, turns to face the chairs, and kneels directly on the concrete floor for prayer.

The tone of the service is reverent but relaxed. The host family provides crackers or cookies for the young children, who are expected to sit quietly through the three-hour service. Children work their way between the women's side of the gathering and the men's, watching, listening, and seeking comfort, as at ease with their fathers as with their mothers. A breastfeeding mother takes her baby to a separate room to feed him; when the infant falls asleep, the mother lays him on a bed and returns to worship.

Another song follows the kneeling prayer, during which people who need a break slip out and return in time for a second minister to preach the longer sermon. That begins just before 11:00 AM and lasts an hour and a half. At the end of this sermon, the preachers ask for testimonies from men in the gathering. Will anyone confirm that today's messages have been true to the Word of God? Two men give witness to the sermons' veracity and importance, elaborating briefly the themes of the messages. A final song rounds out the meeting, and the congregants file out in reverse order.

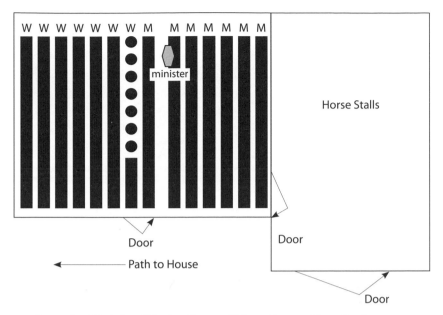

Figure 8.1 Workshop Worship Setting, Holmes County, Ohio, October 2007.

Unhurriedly, the members cross the yard and enter the lower level of the house where our hosts will serve lunch. Built into a hill, the lower level offers a bright, large basement meeting room with white concrete block walls. There are a dozen tables set with flatware, two cups, napkins, and a plate for each place. The men and the women have tables on opposite sides of the room. There are plenty of tables, so everyone but the servers sit at one time to eat together. Matching yellow plastic cafeteria trays placed between every four people offer stacks of sliced turkey, ham, Swiss and American cheeses, homemade white and wheat bread, butter, peanut butter spread, pickled beets, and pickles. Young girls circulate pitchers of lemonade, tea, and water. Next, they pass trays of assorted handmade cookies. If one round isn't enough, the servers return to offer a second helping and follow with more Styrofoam cups and insulated pitchers of coffee.

After the substantial but simple meal, women and men, segregated in worship and at mealtime, socialize separately on porch swings set on the broad two-storied verandas. Men gather on the lower patio and women on the upper, while the teen girls finish the dishes. We visit and laugh. I feel a little like a long-lost cousin at a family reunion, welcomed into the group but trying to figure out who is who. The children nap in an upstairs bedroom, sit quietly among the parents, or go off to play with older sib-lings. Some teens head out to complete chores before the evening singing. A couple of boys ask permission to go swimming. After a while, two fami-lies begin gathering up children and hitching up buggies. My friends will go home later, so I thank the women for their kindness in including me in their circle and excuse myself.

The Meaning of Amish Worship

Singing occupies a critical space in Amish worship life. During worship services, the Amish spend two hours listening to sermons, an hour sing-ing, and only a few minutes praying. Singing reinforces the messages of the Scripture reading and the sermonizing. Because of its reliance on the *Ausbund*, worship singing also serves to connect contemporary Amish be-lievers with the martyrs who went before them. It helps them recognize and admit the parts of themselves that are still unredeemed and in need of transformation, as well as extol the wonders of God's grace toward sinful humans. Singing is cut from the same cloth as the rest of the Amish wor-ship experience, which centers on praise and instruction, admonitions and encouragement.

From childhood to adulthood, Amish people have heard hundreds of hours of meditations on biblical themes from the fall (Adam and Eve's dis-obedience, which led to their expulsion from Eden) to human redemption (by faith in Jesus's self-sacrifice on the cross, reliance on God's Word, and separation from the world). The annually published schedule of Scripture readings sets the topics for preaching. For example, once a year the preach-ing centers on liberty or *Freiheit*, based on John 8 and Galatians 5; another time, the sermon is on the end of the world after Jesus returns, based on Matthew 24 and 25. Amish area bookstores and businesses make the schedule available for about a dollar.

The locus of Amish worship is actually the home, which is consistently seen as the proper place for nurturing children in the faith. Families are strongly encouraged to set aside a time each morning for Scripture reading and prayer. Couples work together to raise a godly family, but the Amish husband leads the family as the head of the household. Because worship of God holds a solemn place in the lives of the Amish, the family as the primary socializing force for Amish children must uphold its role in nur-turing their love of God through worship at home. Families do not necessarily have a prescribed list of Scripture to use. While many New Order families use spontaneous prayers in family worship, Old Order families often choose to use printed prayers from the *Christenpflicht*, a family prayer book first printed in America in 1745 for devotional reading. Some families order devotionals, such as one called *Beside the Still Waters*; others decide to read a chapter of the Bible each day, following this with prayer and singing.

In terms of Sunday worship, then, each Amish district holds worship services every other week in members' homes. In Holmes County, the communing districts (groups that agree on what are considered the "essentials" of faith) divide themselves into A and B groups. All the A groups hold church on one Sunday and the B groups on the following Sunday. On the opposite weeks, members may visit in each other's homes or visit a neighboring service in their area. Because of this schedule, ministers may preach in each other's districts, lending variety in style and substance to reach listeners' hearts in new ways. The Amish do not generally hold extra services on Sunday or Wednesday nights, although the New Order Amish now hold Sunday school sessions on Sundays when worship services are not held. In those sessions, studying the Bible and cementing friendships go hand in hand.

A New Order man explains the meaning of worship to me this way: "Giving yourself to all the Christian people in fellowship is the purpose of worship. We can't be Christians in isolation." His wife adds, "We are in a fold. The others care about you. Worship is a shelter or protection."[1]

We now turn to the role of singing in Amish worship, beginning with the song-like pulpit intonations of Amish ministers and moving to the content and qualities of the *Ausbund*, the hymnal used in Amish worship services.

The Pulpit Intonation

The Amish came to Ohio at the turn of the nineteenth century during the Second Great Awakening, a period in which utopian community life was expanding in Ohio. The Shakers, Owenites, Fourierists, and Mormons, to name only the most prominent, established communities from Kirtland to Cincinnati. The new state of Ohio offered rich, affordable land and a measure of freedom for experimentation. It is difficult to know the extent of Amish awareness of these movements, but one aspect of the Second

Great Awakening that seems to have influenced the Amish is the preaching style. The singing and whooping chants of white and black preachers of this time mixed and mingled in the camp revivals, bringing a new texture to staid, organized religion.[2]

While preaching itself holds the primary position in more progressive Amish orders, another important element of every service is the reading of Scripture. Most ministers now preach and pray in Pennsylvania Dutch but still read the Scriptures in High German. Swartzentruber services center on Scripture reading. "There is not much of a sermon," one Swartzentruber man notes. "There is no English in the service, and the ministers just stand and read a lot of Scripture in High German."[3] Their reasoning centers on their conviction that each believer should receive a message directly from God, not moderated by a human.

To present biblical passages, the preacher may use a pulpit intonation— a kind of sing-song recitative. Most of the notes the minister sings are on the same pitch. He enhances the monotone by leaping from a low note to the pulpit tone at the beginning, stepping up one note and back to the pulpit tone at the end of the phrase, and slowing to allow the congregation time to think about his words (Musical Example 8.1). The minister sings one octave lower than transcribed in the example as he intones the scripture passage, "The Lord is my Shepherd, I shall want for nothing." It sounds like the intense rise and fall of a livestock auctioneer or the preaching style of the rural southern white or African American Baptist preacher.

♩ = 108

Der Herr ist mein Hir - te mir wird nichts man gein   Er wei-det mich auf ein-er grün-en Aue

Musical Example 8.1. Pulpit intonation, Leola, Pennsylvania (1997).

The preacher intones rapidly. The pitch rises to underline important words, putting lively musical emphasis on specific syllables of biblical text. Upper and lower neighboring tones of a whole-step higher (C-sharp) and a half-step lower (A-sharp) encircle the primary tone, a B-natural. Preachers in Pennsylvania are more likely to use the pulpit intonation today than in Ohio. They add another musical way of inviting worshippers to hear the Word of God.

History of the *Ausbund*

It is impossible to describe Amish worship singing without examining the history, contents, and other qualities of the *Ausbund*. The origins of the *Ausbund* are rather sketchy, because its collection developed under what has been called a "shroud of secrecy" to protect its compilers. Notations in the margins of some copies of the hymnbook attribute hymns to leaders of other Protestant groups; for example, hymn 38, "ascribed to John Huss who was burned at the stake in 1415."[4] But between 1537 and 1540, Anabaptist martyrs wrote the nucleus of the hymns—fifty-one, to be exact.[5] One *Ausbund* introduction proclaims, "The following are several other very beautiful hymns composed and sung by the Swiss Brethren in the dungeon of the castle at Passau" where they were incarcerated in southwestern Germany in 1537.[6] They wrote these while awaiting their deaths by hanging, drowning, and burning. These "'*Klagelieder*' [an elegy or complaint] lament their persecution and express love for their persecutors."[7]

With a full 45 stanzas, one of the hymns recounts how a hangman resigned his post rather than participate in an Anabaptist execution, because he admired them. Another *Ausbund* song celebrates the sixteenth-century martyrdom of Elizabeth, a pure, single girl who, although severely tortured, did not recant, only cried out to God. When they were finished with her interrogation, Elizabeth's tormentors drowned her.

In "The Old Order Amish, Their Hymns and Hymn Tunes," English professor John Umble notes that the Anabaptists circulated broadsides, posters tacked to doors for publicizing the message, and later gathered two collections, each of more than fifty hymns.[8] Leaders joined the two collections in 1564 (table 8.1). The larger of the two collections became hymns 3–80; the other collection included what are hymns 81–130 of today's *Ausbund*. Actually, the second set contains the hymns written by the early martyrs. Later Anabaptist publications inserted ten more hymns, including hymn 132, which commemorates the martyrdom of Hans Landis in 1614. In 1571, officials confiscated copies of this forbidden, "heretical," and "dangerous song book" and punished anyone they caught with it. Officials in Bern, Switzerland continued to ban the *Ausbund* for more than one hundred years.[9]

Table 8.1 Chronology of the *Ausbund*

European editions	Hymns	Hymn authors (number)	Publisher	Place of publication
1524	First Anabaptist martyr ballads, hymns 81–130	Hans Koch, Leonhart Meister	—	Printed individually
1564	53 hymns, hymns 3–80	Passau martyrs (51)	Unknown	Switzerland
1583	First *Ausbund* edition: 130 hymns, combines two collections, hymns 3–80 and 81–130 (in current edition)	Swiss Brethren (100), Dutch (11), North German (11), Bohemian Brethren (5), Hutterites ("several")	Unknown	Unknown
1809	Same	Same	von Mechel brothers	Unknown

Source: Ohio Amish Library, *Songs of the* Ausbund, 6, 9, 10; Wolkan, *Die Lieder der Wiedertäufer* (1965), 142–43.

By 1622, adherents to the Anabaptist family had codified the *Ausbund*, producing multiple European editions. Christopher Sauer published the first American edition in Germantown, Pennyslvania, in 1742.[10] This edition contained the original 140 hymns in the main body and 5 additional in an appendix. Liebert and Billymyer's edition in 1785 added one hymn in an appendix. Other American publishers included Joseph Ehrenfried in 1815, Johann Bär and Sons in 1834, and the Mennonite Publishing House in 1880. Publishers continue to reprint the book.[11]

Both the Mennonites and the Amish used the *Ausbund* in the United States until the early nineteenth century. Then, the Mennonites started compiling new hymnals in English and German. The Amish, however, rely on the *Ausbund* even today for worship singing. A few have chosen to sing only the *Ausbund* songs that have been printed in the *Liedersammlung* to eliminate the need for buying two hymnbooks. But most Amish groups employ the *Ausbund* itself in worship.

Texts of the *Ausbund*

The hymn-writing Swiss Brethren wrote the poems of the *Ausbund* to implore members to faithfully endure the persecution frequent in those times.[12] They also wrote to praise God and to elaborate on the doctrines, such as the belief in salvation through grace, evident in forsaking all sin, and practices—such as footwashing during communion celebrations— that they had adopted as normative. Through these hymn texts, they could establish their faith and indoctrinate new members into it.

John Umble, in the article mentioned earlier, describes in depth the contents of the hymns. Some hymns are devotional. Other hymns teach religious doctrines of freedom of religious choice and the law of love of neighbor. Some celebrate the personal qualities of friendliness, forgiveness, patience, and sadness at the evil in the world. The first song in the *Ausbund*, "Obgleich die Harf," gives directions for the proper spiritual attitude during singing. The writer urges, "Christians shall in spirit and truth, sing, pray, and sing psalms":

> *Although the harp is good and sharp,*
> *That rings in the ears,*
> *Still there is no proper sound unless it is tuned,*
> *No string gives its right sound*
> *If one does not strike it rightly,*
> *With free improvisation, according to the fingering chart, .*
> *And on the appropriate frets.*[13]

Worship songs like *Ausbund* 770—"O Gott Vater, wir loben Dich," a praise hymn sung during every worship service—focus on the crucial message of living "in righteousness." We will examine this hymn, which the Amish call the *Loblied* or *Lobsang*, in much more detail in chapter 10. Other song texts exhort:

> The first gift . . . is godly fear / . . . It trembles by God's word, / and enters through the strait gate; / . . . The second gift is goodness which prepares man to love his neighbor heartily (*Ausbund* 275).
>
> Help us out of sin's affliction / . . . Let us not stray from Thee / and no more be like the world (*Ausbund* 408).

Christ the Lord presents to us the doctrine, / the same informs us: work repentence, / follow my footsteps, and shun all sin (*Ausbund* 481).

Show yourself obedient, turn away from evil. / . . . Death has no difference between old and young, If you do not keep yourself in the right, it will be to your sorrow (*Ausbund* 242).

All you Christians who are yielded to God, / Press here and sing with rich sound and with zeal (*Ausbund* 530).

Nothing is sweeter than Christ's yoke (*Ausbund* 180).

Some *Ausbund* hymn texts criticize other Protestant movements, like that of Luther, while setting the norms for Anabaptist life. Personal holiness, they claim, is the test of faith. In *Ausbund* hymn 94, verses 21 and 22, Riall and Peters write that the Anabaptists "put the whole Wittenberg [Lutheran] movement into question by its failure to produce holiness."[14]

True Christians are of this kind, / who live this way / and who bury / all fleshly desires with Christ, / who are led by God's Spirit / to the host of angels / so that they touch no evil. / He will protect them from sin.

Now I will tell further / also about the Church of Sin, / which boasts much with words / how they are good Christians. / They all say they believe, / but with their deeds / they certainly deny it. / I consider it illusion.[15]

Amish writers have also tried to identify, based on their texts, *Ausbund* hymns borrowed from medieval folksongs. For example, *Ausbund* 70 resembles a fifteenth-century song starting with the same lines:

Text of Ausbund 70:	*Medieval Folksong:*
Fröhlich so will ich singen,	Fröhlich so will ich singen,
Mit Lust ein Tageweiss,	Mit Lust ein Tageweiss,
Von wunderlichen Dingen,	Ich hoff, mir sol gelingen,
Dem höchsten Gott zu Preiss,	Darauf leg ich mein Fleiss,
In seinem Namen heb ich an,	Gegen einem Frewlein reich,
Sein Gnad woll er mir günen,	Auf einer Burg so hoch.
So g'lingt mirs auf der Bahn.	

This comparison shows that at least some *Ausbund* texts derive from the lyrics of secular songs of the time, which writers molded into texts appropriate for and conducive to worship. Amish people agree that some of the tunes they use for *Ausbund* hymns also came from those folksongs.

Ausbund Tunes

Since no copies of the *Ausbund* include musical notes, and since, of course, there are no recordings of Amish tunes from the sixteenth century, the evolution of the tunes of the *Ausbund* proves much more difficult to ascertain than the evolution of the texts. The tunes were actually of little importance to the Anabaptists; they functioned only to enhance the words and to make them easier to remember.

In his book *Four Hundred Years with the* Ausbund, Paul Yoder cites Joseph W. Yoder and George Pullen Jackson's research to assert that the *Ausbund* tunes include secular folk tunes "familiar to all of the singers," sixteenth-century chorale melodies taken from Gregorian chants, sacred folksongs, and those composed for use both in the Roman Catholic church and by the followers of Reformation leader John Calvin.[16] These researchers conclude that "many of the tunes first adopted for use in the *Ausbund* are still used today."[17] The Amish have added many embellishments to the tunes, probably during the nineteenth century. Lacking a director, the group singing caused each tune to be "dragged out, which led to many kinds of strange ornamentation, which were foreign to the original tune," *Ausbund* researcher Paul Yoder explains.[18]

According to Rudolf Wolkan, who studied Anabaptist hymns in 1903, "Only three [tunes are] thought to be original tunes by Anabaptist composers": Georg Wagner, Wolff Gernold, and Ludwig Hätzer.[19] For texts that could not be sung to those tunes, the Anabaptists borrowed well-known folk tunes or religious melodies, many of which were written by priest-reformer Martin Luther, such as "Ein feste Burg ist unser Gott."[20] The *Ausbund* lists eighty-two tune names, fifty-six of which have been identified by Wolkan, including twenty-six spiritual songs and thirty folk tunes.[21]

The tune of the song about the young martyr Elizabeth, mentioned earlier, is known as "Magdelein." It actually serves as the tune for several *Ausbund* hymns, including the favorite of an Old Order Amish woman with whom I spoke (Musical Example 8.2).

In the first phrase, the beauty of the melody stems from the swell of the four-note rise on "O" (at A) to the three-note rise on "*Schöp-*" (at B) and the

Musical Example 8.2. "O Gott Schöpfer," Wayne County (2008).
Source: Unidentified Amish woman, personal interview, March 2008.
Translation: *O God Creator, Holy Spirit!*
To Your praise and glory most of all
In unity we want to sing,
And strive after the good gifts.

gentle fall as the melody rounds out each phrase in a sequence from "*Hei-*" (at C) repeated on "*-ger*" (at D) to "*Geist*" (at E). The melody peaks on the second note of the second phrase, rising from G-sharp to A, and then recedes to the opening B. Interestingly, this melody never uses a D but skips over that note each time.

Singing *Ausbund* tunes is not easy. Many of the syllables of text have five or more notes. Musicians call the melody melismatic when three or more notes are sung for one syllable of text. One song, "O Vater, steh uns gnädig bei," has seventeen syllables sung with four notes each, three with five notes, three with six notes, and seven with seven notes. Because the group sings all of these in unison, this takes substantial concentration and practice.

All *Ausbund* songs proceed at a very slow pace. The Amish explain the speed as a change the early Anabaptists made when other prisoners danced to their singing. Because they believed that dancing was not an appropriate activity, slowing their singing down made the tune impossible to dance to. In some ways, the speed allows beginners to join in tentatively and, over many Sundays, learn where the tune goes.

Another factor that makes the *Ausbund* tunes difficult is the wide vocal range of many of the hymns. For congregational singing in Christian denominations, most hymns span an octave or less. For example, the familiar Christmas song "Joy to the World" spans one octave. If it is started at high C and falls to middle C, most singers can comfortably sing all eight notes. By contrast, think of the many times individuals and groups have failed to sing many of the notes of "The Star-Spangled Banner," a tune that spans an octave and a fifth, 12 notes! A survey of the tunes from Wayne and Holmes counties collected by Ben Troyer, Jr., shows that almost three times as many tunes span an octave or greater as those of less than an octave.[22] This means that some voices will have to strain—or practice regularly to stretch their vocal chords—in order to reach all the notes.

Rehearsing the Old Tunes

Musicologists writing in the mid-twentieth century remarked that, when they attended worship gatherings, it was not unusual for the Amish to stop in the middle of the service for a singing practice.[23] The fear that the old melodies will be lost continues, but today there are few worship gathering rehearsals. Instead, the practices take the shape of men's gatherings several days before worship services. One man says he meets with a group about once a month during the winter, when the men's outdoor workload is lighter. In another district, New Order Amishman Atlee Miller explains, "We do not have men's sings. All the married men in our district are *Vorsingers* but one. He says he will learn them. I know the Old Order Amish men in Holmes County gather on the Friday nights before worship Sunday every other week when they are available."[24]

At these sings, the men rehearse the hymns they will sing on subsequent Sundays and review the more commonly sung *Ausbund* tunes, repeating difficult lines over and over until everyone gets them right. Older men judge when a younger man has gained the proficiency and confidence to lead a certain song. On Sunday morning, a *Vorsinger* will give the younger man—a teenager even—the nod and that young man will spontaneously lead the singing, with support if necessary.

Even with all these efforts, supplemental notes sneak in. John Umble quotes Goshen College professor Walter E. Yoder: "When one hears an Amish congregation sing these tunes, he notes that there is freedom in the interpretation of the melody. One hears passing notes and embellishments in some voices, not all. This practice, no doubt, is a carry-over from the ancient method of singing plainsong chants."[25] Yoder sees freedom, not conformity. Sometimes others in the congregation pick up these added notes, and they become standardized into the community singing.

A group of Amish in Holmes County has finished the second in a pair of translations of *Ausbund* hymns from German to English to promote greater understanding of the meanings behind these hymns. These translators agree with Amish scholar Umble that "singing probably did more to make the Reformation a popular movement than did the reading of the New Testament."[26] The martyrs wrote to encourage their children and friends to stay true to their convictions despite cruel, torturous persecutions, loss of life and home, and exile. Moreover, singing the *Ausbund* hymns helps the Amish to maintain their identity and buttresses the Amish community.

Amish life revolves around praise and worship, and the *Ausbund* furnishes the songs for worship. Children and youth attend worship services throughout their childhood and teen years. In their late teens or into their twenties, the youth must decide for themselves whether they will commit themselves to God in baptism and become full-fledged, voting, and communing adult members of their districts or whether they will choose the wide road. Next, we will discuss the songs of belonging sung in the services in which the Amish receive new members and celebrate communion, a commemorative service based on Jesus's Last Supper.

CHAPTER 9

Songs of Belonging
Baptism, Council, and Communion

Ach, wann ich ja gedenk daran,	*Oh, when I stop to think upon*
Wie viele sund ich hab gethan,	*How many sins that I have done.*
Wie oft ich meinen Gott betrübt,	*How often I my God have grieved,*
Und er mich doch so herzlich liebt.	*And yet He loves me heartily.*

—*Eine Unparteiische Liedersammlung* (1892/1999)

My hostess has just finished showing me the white-on-white quilts of flowers, birds, and horses that she makes from her own designs. "When I was going through, I was with two girls who were a little wild," says this active seventy-year-old Amish woman as she begins to tell me about preparing for church membership. We sip tea at her kitchen table. "[The congregation] made us wait an extra two weeks before they would approve us."[1] Joining the church was a promise she made about fifty years ago and one that she has kept diligently since that time. She supports her friends and neighbors, attends worship services, and has raised five children, all of whom have joined the church themselves. But now, reflecting back on her younger years, she smiles at me across the table. "My bonnet did have too many pleats," she admits, a twinkle in her eye.

Joining church is a ritual of belonging in the lives of young adults who decide that they are ready to take on the responsibilities and commitments of church membership. The next step after deciding is baptism. The baptism service, along with council meetings and communion services, is a special event in the Amish church calendar and underscores the communal nature of Amish worship and life. Singing plays a critical role in each of these services.

Joining Church

Baptism, or "joining church," is a key step in the life of an Amish young person. The Amish believe that humans are born with a sinful nature and must repent. They base this belief specifically on John 3 and Romans 6:3– 4. Since the Amish believe that candidates for baptism must be old enough to understand the seriousness of the commitment they are making, Amish parents do not encourage children and younger youth to seek membership. One of the essential tenets of their faith, which stood in direct contradiction to the infant baptism practiced by the state church during the earliest years of the Anabaptist movement, is adult confessing, also called "believer" baptism.

After the spring communion service, youth preparing to join the church attend eight or nine classes with the ministers, one each week on Sunday afternoons in some fellowships or during the worship hour plus at Sunday school time in others. The baptismal preparation entails studying the eighteen articles from the Dordrecht Confession, written in 1632 by a peace convention of a ministers' group in Dordrecht, Holland. These articles amount to an Amish catechism that describes the doctrines concerning important issues such as repentance and redemption, Christian marriage, swearing an oath, and maintaining a nonviolent lifestyle. After the ninth time of instruction, the minister may recommend the youth to the members for a vote. Sometimes, they are ready earlier—or later.

A youth whose parents have been contentious may have a harder time being approved for baptism. "Parents' lives influence their children's, don't they?" one Amish person queried.[2] The third time the youth goes out for instruction, the ministers ask the assembled district members to observe the candidates to see if they show evidence of "new birth." Have the youths' lives shown evidence of a change in their spirits?

For the baptism, parents customarily give their youth new clothes to represent their new birth. Girls joining the church wear fresh white caps and aprons, symbols of purity. Boys receive a *mutza* coat with a "flapper," or split-seam pleat, in the back seam, required dress for adult male church members. Church garb for the boys and men is white shirts, although they may wear a variety of blues and purples at other times. Commonality of dress emphasizes unity and their new status as adult members.

By late July or early August, and two weeks after a unanimously favorable vote, those approved are ready for baptism and joining church. At the regular Sunday morning service, the selected scripture passages center on baptism, and both ministers preach on this theme. One New Order group sings four verses of "Ach, wann ich ja" ("O, When I Think of My Many Sins") from the *Liedersammlung* as the third song of the service and the last four verses after the actual baptism.[3] They use the tune of "Saffron Walden," also used for "Just As I Am," composed by Arthur Henry Brown in 1890[4] (see appendix I, Musical Example A1.18).

After the usual preaching, interspersed with singing, the bishop asks the candidates several questions and the candidates kneel, signifying their choice of committing to God's guidance and the community's correction. Each answers four questions, including, "Do you believe that Jesus is the Son of God?" An older woman or "sister" in the gathering removes each girl's head covering. The bishop holds his hands over the head of each youth and gives a blessing as a minister pours water from a cup through the bishop's cupped hands—"In the name of the Father," one splash, "and of the Son," again, "and of the Holy Ghost," a third stream of water. As the bishop slowly opens his palms, the water cascades gently over the hair and face of each youth, one by one. The sister replaces the girls' coverings. The minister or bishop gives the boys a hand to rise and gives each a light kiss of greeting on the lips, welcoming them into the body of believers and fulfilling the instruction attributed to Peter, "Greet one another with a holy kiss."[5] The sister greets the girls similarly. Following several more admonitions to the young members, statements of witness from men in the congregation, and a prayer, the minister announces the Scripture lessons for the following service—two weeks away—expecting that each member will read and study the Scripture to prepare for hearing the Word. The service closes with *Ausbund* hymn 655, and the group adjourns to eat lunch.

The ritual of "joining church" adds extra time to a worship service. In 2005, because of unusually high temperatures, the preachers shortened the baptismal service in one community—that is, they added only one extra hour, a woman recalls.

Council Meetings

Remembrances of Jesus's Last Supper occur twice a year for the Amish—in the spring, near Easter, and six months later in the fall, sometime between early September and early October. If regular worship services are vital events of Amish life, communion is an even more heightened one.

Two weeks before communion, the district holds a members-only council meeting following the midday meal where adult members meet to affirm or refine the *Ordnung*. On these Sundays, nonmembers attend a neighboring fellowship meeting or stay at home. That day's service might be abbreviated but all parts are included, including sermons and singing. They sing "O Herre Gott in deinem Thron" at this special service. The bishop sermonizes on the Hebrew prophets, leading to an exhortation on the rules of the church. After lunch, members convene to discuss concerns related to the *Ordnung*, to review the members' adherence to the rules, and to act on urging backsliders to curtail egregious infractions. If there is disagreement on any proposed new rules or alterations to existing ones, the group must continue to work through to consensus. Staying out of fellowship would not make it possible for them to be ready to commune together. When they all agree, they schedule communion for the Sunday worship two weeks later.

The Amish express compassion for those who fall or break away. Their family prayer book, *Christenpflicht*, includes prayers for backsliders.[6] During the council meeting, a fallen brother or sister may confess and find a welcome from the group. One related *Ausbund* hymn includes these lyrics:

> *All men are guilty*
> *Of their sins before God,*
> *If He grants them His favor,*
> *It happens through grace alone;*
> *It is not earned by works—*
> *It is compassion.*
> *Man shall also take note*
> *Of the basic and true instruction,*
> *How he may come back*
> *To God's grace and favor.*
> *So that he may be accepted,*

His debt be forgiven.
He shall bear great sorrow and grief
In his heart
On account of his sins
Which he has committed.[7]

For smaller sins, the sinner may talk to God in private. But for more serious transgressions that affect the whole community, the Amish believe that the individual should repent publicly. Also, if the group has excommunicated an individual for repeated disregard of the *Ordnung* and the person seeks reinstatement, the penitent kneels before the congregation to confess. Anyone who refuses to repent is excluded from communion.[8]

Communion

Preaching in the communion service focuses on the life of Christ, from the prophecy of his birth through his resurrection. Scripture reading, sermonizing, singing, and prayers abound. These elements are interspersed with the breaking of the bread, sharing of the cup of wine, and footwashing, all of which reenact Christ's Last Supper.[9] Footwashing, practiced by only a few Christian groups these days but emphasized by Jacob Amman, symbolizes mutual surrender, care, and responsibility to other believers. A New Order bishop asserts that anyone who has left the church will not be shunned if he attends a church that has "all the parts of communion," which means it includes footwashing.

Two often-used communion songs are: "Von Herzen woll'n wir singen" (Musical Example 9.1) and "O Gott Vater ins Himmels Throne" (see appendix I, Musical Example A1.8).

Both of these songs are melismatic, with many notes per syllable, as is apparent in the example above. Melismatic chant allows the singers much time to concentrate on every word; in this particularly somber service, the style matches the weighty content of a time of remembrance. The Amish believe that remembrance of Christ's work of salvation encourages believers in their faith walk. Striving to be like Christ remains the main message of the communion service.

These special services—baptism, council meeting, and communion—emphasize the sense of responsibility and belonging, which the community nurtures in Amish community members from childhood. Through

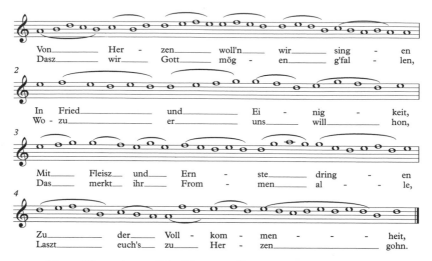

Musical Example 9.1. "Von Herzen woll'n wir singen," Troyer (1997).
Translation: *We want to sing from the heart*
In peace and unity,
With diligence and earnestness
To press toward perfection,
So that we may please God,
Towards God's purpose for us,
Note this, all you godly people,
Let it go to your hearts.

these, worship combines with maintenance of the community in decision making, confession, restoration of relationships, and celebration of fellowship. As mentioned previously, the Amish also view worship as the human's natural response to a loving God, who alone is worthy of praise and adoration. The Amish sing the *Lobsang*, to which we now turn our attention, in every bi-weekly worship service. This song manifests the centrality of praise in Amish life and also provides an excellent example of the continuity of a hymn text and tune in various locations over a long stretch of time.

CHAPTER 10

Case Study: The *Loblied*, or *Lobsang*

O Gott Vater, wir loben Dich,	*O God Father, we glorify Thee*
Und Deine Güte preisen,	*And Thy goodness praise.*
Dass Du Dich, o Herr, gnädiglich,	*That Thou Thyself O Lord graciously*
An uns neu hast bewiesen,	*To us anew has manifested*
Und hast uns, herr, zusammen g'führt,	*And hast us Lord together led*
Uns zu ermahnen durch Dein Wort,	*Us to admonish through Thy Word*
Gib uns Genad zu diesem.	*Give us grace to this.*

—*Ausbund* (1564/1997)

Hilde Binford sings the *Loblied* in a clear voice as we enjoy breakfast together at a highway truck stop. Binford teaches musicology at Moravian College in Bethlehem, Pennsylvania, near the heart of the first Amish settlement in colonial America. "I know the whole thing from memory," she boasts, beaming. She has mastered the *Loblied* by singing in worship services beside her Amish friends.

Learning the *Loblied*, "O Gott Vater, wir loben Dich," is no mean feat. Singers sing from the *Ausbund*, which contains only the text. They have to learn the melody by heart. One syllable may have as many as eight notes. And one verse, with about 225 notes and taking five minutes or more to sing, is almost twice as long as an entire popular music selection—with no instrumental accompaniment to help with the pitch and momentum. So with all four verses, the *Loblied* can take twenty or more minutes for the congregation to sing. Sung slowly, the *Loblied*, sometimes referred to as the *Lobsang* or *Lobgesang*, offers an opportunity for meditation and worship. The simple melody moves with a lithe grace, and the message of the text underscores the Amish desire to direct their gaze toward the Almighty.

Whereas the other hymns change from service to service, the *Loblied* is always the second song sung at bi-weekly worship services. It thus occupies the most privileged place of any hymn on the Amish musical landscape. After congregants have completed the opening hymn in Sunday worship, the ministers and bishop rise and leave the gathering for the *Abrot*, the ministers' meeting during which they decide who will preach in the service and share counsel on other issues facing the community. The worshipers continue the service in the leaders' absence by singing the *Loblied*.

"We sing this song every Sunday," explains an Old Order man. David and his mother, Naomi, sing the first verse for me. David starts each line, and they stagger their breathing for the remainder of the line to produce a continuous sound. "In worship services there are more of us; we don't run out of breath," adds his mother. David is an experienced singer but leads the second line and succeeding lines a half pitch higher than the first. "I can follow, but I can't lead the *Ausbund* tunes myself," Naomi admits. In the sixth line of the song, she misses the melody and goes off on her own. David suggests that this sometimes happens in worship. "Last Sunday we had a lot of visitors in the service. We asked several [of the men] to each lead one line of the *Loblied* as a way of welcoming them. Sometimes, they got off and we came in to try to get them back on," David explains. "The sixth line is especially hard." He refers to the only line with an accidental, a note outside the given key, which raises the fourth note in the scale a half step. "We sang it a bit faster than we do in worship," he also admits. "It usually takes us twenty minutes to do all four verses."

David and Naomi's descriptions of the variations that occur in the singing of the *Loblied* are indicative of the ways that this hymn has been stretched through time and region, all without losing its shape. A close examination of the *Loblied* provides a fascinating window into Amish worship life and the musical practices that so heavily form it. We look first at the history of the text and tune of this central praise hymn and then turn to a discussion of how it is sung and notated in a variety of contexts.

Origins of the *Loblied*

The Amish sing the *Loblied* from the *Ausbund* with words that were written 450 years ago. According to Rudolf Wolkan in *Die Lieder der Wiedertäufer*, Leenaert Clock of Holland, a prolific author credited with over four hundred hymns, wrote the text of the *Loblied* in 1525.[1] The text asserts that, although the faithful suffer sorrow and loneliness, they may lean on God and count on God's presence. In gratitude for God's constancy, believers seek to praise God for granting them wisdom and truth and for leading them to a holy, pious life. The hymn reveals much about the Amish belief that praise of God is the primary aim of humans.

The melody of the *Loblied*, like melodies of other *Ausbund* hymns, corresponds to a secular tune, "Es wollt ein Magdlein Wasser hollen," which the Anabaptists also adopted for the text "Aus tiefer Not schrei ich zu Dir," beginning about 1534.[2]

The Amish relate that their melodies have been passed down through the generations, but it is impossible to tell whether they are the same as those first sung by the martyrs and early Anabaptists. This study of the *Loblied* demonstrates a strong consistency in the melodies the Amish have sung from 1930 through the early twenty-first century. By examining several sung and notated versions of the *Loblied*, we can identify regional and historical variations in the melody as well as striking commonalities among them.

Holmes County, Ohio, Version

A Holmes County singer demonstrates the hymn (Musical Example 10.1) by singing one verse. At the pace she chooses, the four verses of the song would take only twelve minutes to sing. She acknowledges that she was singing it much faster than usual because of her nervousness and unfamiliarity with singing this song alone—and into a tape recorder. The nuances of the turns of the notes (gliding here, solid there, stronger then lighter), the lilt, the sweetness of her voice, the intensity, the sincerity of purpose—none of these can be adequately described or diagrammed. Suffice it to say, while the song may appear lethargic on paper, there is energy and melodic interest within each phrase when one hears it sung. In the worship setting, hearing the voices attune themselves to the others adds aesthetic satisfaction.

In this version of the *Loblied*, the Holmes County singer elongates several notes in each line and scoops and slides into and out of notes.[3] Other singers singing the same song do not. Naomi takes frequent breaths within one line, almost one for each word. But as Naomi previously pointed out, a group would stagger their breathing so that no obvious pauses would be heard. This *Loblied* melody employs repetition as an organizing principle;

Musical Example 10.1. "Loblied," Holmes County (October 2006).
Translation: (verse 1) O God Father, we glorify Thee,
And Thy goodness praise;
That Thou Thyself O Lord graciously,
To us anew hast manifested.
And hast us Lord together led
Us to admonish through Thy Word,
Give us grace to this.
(verse 2) Open the mouth Lord (of) Thy servants
Give them wisdom besides
That they Thy Word may speak correctly
What serves to (a) pious life
And useful is to Thy praise
Give us hunger after such food
This is our desire.

Musical Example 10.1. (continued)
(verse 3) Give our hearts also understanding
Enlightenment here on earth
That thy Word in us become known
That we pious may become
And live in righteousness
Heeding on Thy Word all-times
So remains man undeceived.
(verse 4) Thine, O Lord, is the kingdom alone
And also the power altogether
We praise Thee in the church
And thank Thy name
And beseech Thee from hearts-depth
Wouldst by us be in this hour
Through Jesus Christ, Amen.

for example, several lines are repeated exactly (lines 1, 2, and 7 are the same, and lines 3 and 4 match). Lines 2, 4, and 6 start on D and end on C. Line 7 starts on C and also ends on C (table 10.1 has more detail).

The melody is almost thoroughly *diatonic,* containing the notes that make up the major scale, except for one accidental, an F-sharp in line 6, third note. In the entire melody, she sings only one F sharp, which is the

Table 10.1 The *Loblied's* melodic structure

Line of melody	Description	Notes per syllable	Opening/ final note
1, 2		6/5	G/E, D/C*
3, 4	Opening G becomes A in 3rd line	6/5	A/E, D/C*
	Repeats lines 1, 2 with some rhythmic irregularity		
5	Similar to 4th, one step lower	5	C/A
	No text painting or textual reason for melodic rises and falls, "And hast us Lord together led"		
6	"Zu er," moves by thirds, G triad, D-B-G (below middle C), reverses and sings G-B-D, change from previous step-wise movement	5	D/C*
7	Repeats line 2 with rhythmic changes	5	C/C*

* When final C, C anticipates.

sole note foreign to the C scale. In the ascending melody, the effect of raising the F to F-sharp makes the E–F-sharp a wider interval, a step rather
than a half step.[4] No Amish person could explain why they sharped this
note. The melody has come to them this way. There is no obvious melodic
or textual reason for this accidental note, but it also appears in a 1997
Holmes County, Ohio, version in print (in Musical Example 10.2, see the
third note of the melisma on the syllable "Uns"). In the Troyer version
there are three Fs in line 6, and it is not clear whether all three are sharped.
The Holmes County version (Musical Example 10.1) uses only the first
two sharps. The melody line varies on both the "-nen" of "ermahnen" and
on "durch." The F-sharp does not, however, appear in a 1929 version from
Pennsylvania. This change documents one very unusual and surprising
melodic variant, an F-sharp instead of an F, between 1929 and 1997.

Musical Example 10.2. "Loblied," Lomax, Southeastern Iowa, part 1.
Source: Umble, "The Old Order Amish," 93.

The *Loblied* melody is largely *pentatonic*, employing only five notes of
the scale C-D-E-F-G. Of the 225 notes sung for each verse, only 14 are
outside this group: seven As and six Bs, each below the middle C, and the
single F-sharp above middle C.

The *Loblied* in the Troyer Edition

The second version of the *Loblied* (Musical Example 10.2) comes from the
Troyer shape-note songbook edition called Ausbund *and* Liedersammlung *Songs*. There is no clef sign designating the starting pitch. The group
can make any note *do*, the first note of the major scale (as in the song "Doe,
a deer") and in this case the starting and main note. This allows the leader
to choose the most comfortable range for the assembled group.

Several tune inconsistencies are noticeable between the Holmes County
and Troyer versions. As the Holmes County singer begins, she starts with
a low G, or *sol* below the *do*, and slides up to the *do*, whereas the Troyer
version begins directly on the *do* as designated by a triangle. The Holmes
County singer holds some notes for a beat and others for only part of a beat,

with up to four notes on one beat. The Troyer version is written with even beats, all of the same note length. But that is not the way the tune would ever be sung. It is sung more rhythmically, like the Holmes County version (Musical Example 10.1).

Surprisingly, the Troyer uses a text borrowed from the *Ausbund* hymn number 131 for line 3, "Die du, o Herr, so gnädiglich," which emphasizes the love God graciously gives, in place of the Holmes County line "Dass Du Dich, O Herr, gnädiglich," which underlines God, who gives the love. This comparison shows that the text has changed a little over 450 years, but there have been a few more melodic changes.

Lomax Versions of the *Loblied*

Two *Loblied* versions recorded by musicologist Alan Lomax and his wife, Elizabeth, on a Smithsonian Institution–sponsored tour through Iowa and Indiana in 1938, offer snapshots of Amish singing to compare with today's renditions (compare Musical Examples 10.3 [Iowa] and 10.4 [Indiana]).

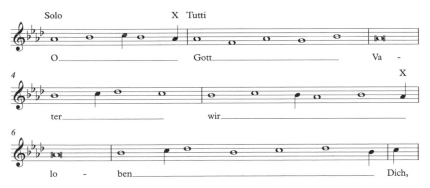

Musical Example 10.3. "Loblied," Lomax, Indiana, Library of Congress 1, part 1 (1938b). Sung by Eli Bontrager and John Oesch of Middlebury, Indiana, 13 April 1938, for Alan Lomax. Transcription by Frey, "Hymns as Folk Music," 156.

The Indiana melody starts a half-step higher. The Iowa version has more complex rhythms, using a mixture of different note values from whole notes to sixteenth notes, while the Indiana version only uses slow (whole notes) and fast (quarter notes). (For a comparison of the openings of each of these versions and the Holmes County and Troyer renditions, see appendix I, Musical Example A1.9.)

Comparing these 1938 written versions of the *Loblied* with the 2006 Holmes County version demonstrates that there is a remarkable consistency among versions from 1938 to 2006, far outweighing minor variations. A few added notes lead to minor melodic differences, but more surprisingly, many congruencies exist between the 1938 and 2006 versions, amazing given the chronological and geographic distance between the communities singing the two versions.

Having said that, the Amish have not retained complete uniformity of the song throughout the years or across the miles. Many rhythmic differences, caused by how long the singer or singing group holds each note, do exist.[5] One striking melodic difference between the Lomax (Musical Example 10.3) and the Holmes County (Musical Example 10.1) version is the addition of anticipatory notes in nearly every line of the Holmes County version. A few anticipations appear in the Indiana version, but none appear in the Iowa rendition. Another difference in the melody of the second syllable of "Va-ter," transposed in C, is that the Lomax version employs D-E-F-E, while the Holmes County melody is D-F-E-D.

The *Loblied* in Mifflin County, Pennsylvania

In 1942, Joseph W. Yoder's landmark collection of Amish hymns, found and notated in the Kishacoquillas Valley of Mifflin County in western Pennsylvania, purports to show the "old way." Yoder's aim was to help Amish families rehearse *Ausbund* hymns at home and to learn, by the use of shape notes, how to sing the old hymns. He expected this practice to improve the singing of the *Ausbund* hymns in community worship services and gave directions for their performance:

All the notes between two consecutive bars are sung to one syllable. This necessitates slurring throughout the entire piece, and as slurring is one of the characteristics of these tunes, the marks indicating slurs are omitted, but understood. The whole notes represent a sustaining of the voice almost as long as a whole note in 2/2 time; the half note somewhat shorter; and the quarter note a quick swing of the voice, a mere touch of the voice to that note; and the double notes represent a rather long sustaining of the voice. A slight stress of the voice on the first part of each syllable is probably as near to the accent as we can come, as there is little if any accent.[6]

These approximations of note lengths reinforce the notion that members practice and learn note lengths by repeatedly singing the songs together. Singers adapt to the group. Indeed, the group must make musical decisions together, since the *Ausbund* contains no musical notations.

Yoder's version of the *Loblied* (Musical Example 10.4) follows an earlier Mifflin County notation of the song, published around 1929 in a book about Mennonite immigration.[7] Yoder uses slightly different, generally longer notes on some pitches and a different key, A-flat major, rather than the G major of the Mifflin version. Otherwise, the melody is the same. Either a *Vorsinger* in Mifflin County used the earlier written version as his guide, or the Amish remained perfectly consistent through those thirteen years.

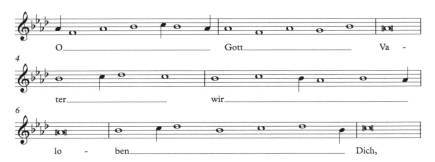

Musical Example 10.4. "Loblied," Yoder, *Amische Lieder* (1942). Sung by
Eli Bontrager and John Oesch of Middlebury, Indiana, 13 April 1938, for
Alan Lomax. Transcription by Frey, "Hymns as Folk Music," 1.

I have yet to find a Holmes County family that owns the Yoder collection, but they would like to. Upon the request of an Amish bishop, I made him a copy from the library book when I couldn't locate an actual book for him.

Leola, Pennsylvania, Version of the *Loblied*

In Leola, Pennsylvania (1997), a group of Amish record another melody for the *Loblied*. As an unusual addition, one *woman* sings harmony in this recording, mostly a third below the man who sings the melody (Musical Example 10.5).

Other than the hymn text, the similarities between this version and the previous one include the same five-note voice range. This is a "fast"

Musical Example 10.5. "Loblied," Leola, Pennsylvania (1997). Source: *Amish Music Variety*, audio CD of an unidentified Old Order Amish group recorded at Harmonies Workshop.

tune, not like any of the tunes used for *Ausbund* singing. Some typical aspects of Amish *Ausbund* singing employed in this version include cutting off the last syllable of the line abruptly, extremely slow tempos, and brief pauses between lines before the *Vorsinger* begins the next line. The melody moves in whole and half steps, with occasional thirds and rarer fourths as the congregants unite in the steady rise and fall of phrases. The harmony is a major element that distinguishes this version from others, but the harmony would not be acceptable in worship services.

One Last Version

Atlee Miller, a Holmes County *Vorsinger*, enjoys talking about singing. Sandwiched between his discussions of singing for special days, he remarks, "We sang a different melody for the *Loblied* when I was a boy." That was nearly seventy years ago (Musical Example 10.6). This information was a significant breakthrough. How many other melodies have the Amish tried and discarded? How many other groups knew or used this alternate melody? Since the Amish have not put emphasis on the melodies, the dominant ones seem to win out, while others drop from usage.

Atlee's great musical memory, along with frequent rehearsal and inter-est in Amish singing, makes him an invaluable resource for documenting changes as well as recovering obsolete melodies.

Musical Example 10.6. "Loblied," Holmes County (ca. 1937).

Whither the *Loblied*?

No one knows how this consummate Amish hymn will evolve or stay the same in the minds and mouths of future generations. The youth in some communities are expressing a strong interest in memorizing the tunes and mastering the singing of hymns such as the *Loblied*. Judging from the strik-ing continuity of the *Loblied*'s melody, text, and rhythm through history, despite some historical and regional variations, we can surmise that the *Loblied* will carry its graceful, solemn tones far into the centuries to come.

PART IV

❧ SINGING FOR SPECIAL OCCASIONS ☙

Songs of Love and Life
Weddings and Funerals

Die Braut geht in den Garten,	*The bride goes into the garden,*
Ein Kron ist ihr bereit,	*A crown is prepared for her,*
Ihr's Bräut'gams will sie warten,	*Her bridegroom will she await,*
Abziehen ihr tötlich Kleid.	*Removing her mortal garb.*
Sie zeucht sich ab von dieser Welt,	*She separates herself from this world,*
Ihr Bräut'gams ist ihr lieber,	*Her bridegroom is more beloved to her,*
Dann alles Gut und Geld.	*Than all goods and money.*

—*Songs of the* Ausbund (1998)

An Amish mother and daughter sit outside on the bright August morning, deboning stewed chicken. They are preparing for the daughter Laura's wedding day, about a month off. As they prepare the chicken for the dressing, Laura and her mother tell me that they have to get a head start in order to be ready to feed more than five hundred guests. A few hundred yards away from where we sit, the men are scraping and painting the barn. Fortunately, they have a rented cherry-picker crane, which is easier to use than scaffolding. "I don't know how we'll get everything done," Laura wonders as she watches them.

Laura is marrying a man who lives less than two miles away, and she will continue to have the support and company of her own family during her married life. Her husband-to-be has started his own business and feels prepared for family responsibility. The Amish believe that marriage is God's plan for humans, that the family is the sanctioned unit, and that the husband should be the head and the wife, his helper.

Amish weddings are celebrations of the highest order. They serve as both family reunions and brief vacations. Youth travel all over the country to act as servers for friends' and relatives' wedding meals, turning weddings themselves into events at which single young men and women can meet potential marriage partners. One Ohio Amish woman in her twenties met a man at a Kentucky wedding, she tells me, and a year later he asked her to marry him. With so many familial and relational connections between districts and settlements, many Amish people have numerous invitations each year. "We went to eight weddings this fall," one Amish grandmother discloses.

Amish weddings are clearly worship services, and funerals are, too. As such, both ceremonies follow many of the musical conventions of the Amish bi-weekly services. As we have seen throughout this exploration of Amish music, singing accompanies many of the activities of daily life among the Amish, and ceremonies of matrimony and remembrance occasion a variety of possibilities. We will examine an Amish wedding first, and then a funeral, to discover how these solemn ceremonies utilize singing—or, in the case of some funerals, preclude singing—to mark them as hallowed, sacred events.

Wedding Music

At the end of September, Laura's wedding day dawns beautifully cool. The family has invited over five hundred people, and all of them come. After more than a month of preparation, two head cooks organize the meal, assigning a job to each helper. Next to the barn, the cooks use a rented refrigerator trailer, stocked with a full kitchen of four stoves, a warmer, a freezer, a refrigerator, and flatware for 350. "The Old Order use real plates. We [New Order] use paper. It's much easier," explains Mary. For this particular wedding, the young married people work together, husbands carrying the heavy pans. Involving husbands in preparing the meal is relatively new, someone tells me, adding that the young couples find they enjoy serving together.

The hostlers (horse minders) tie the buggy horses to two wagons stationed in a field near the large shed where the family will celebrate the wedding service. Quite a few non-Amish friends come, so they have set aside a car park near the broiler chicken house.

The bride has decorated the worship space with flowers and candles. "Weddings are becoming much more elaborate than they once were,"

Grandpa Atlee reminisces, thinking back to his own wedding more than fifty years ago. The bride wears a new dusty blue dress with a white cape and a white head covering, and her attendants wear matching Amish dresses. As an honor, the couple chooses an immediate family member—a father, brother, or grandfather—as *Vorsinger* for the worship service.

Amish wedding days are generally bookended by music. On the morning of Laura's wedding, a dozen or so men and women gather to sing by 8:30. They sing *Ausbund* and *Liedersammlung* songs appropriate to weddings. Weddings are a community time, and close relatives enjoy being together and singing praise to God. Their presence does not serve to entertain the gatherers but sets the tone in order that those who arrive feel invited to participate in the solemnity and joy surrounding a wedding service. The community has a large stake in building strong families committed to God's will. "The wedding isn't the important thing," says bishop Jacob Beachy. "It's the marriage that is important." The point of the wedding is to prepare the couple to take seriously their responsibility to God, one another, and their future children.

People drift in until about ten o'clock, at which time the service begins. Generally, a wedding service lasts almost three hours and includes multiple sermons and the singing of several *Ausbund* songs, just like other worship events. The wedding has about the same tenor as worship: a blend of joy and solemnity.

During the wedding ceremony itself, the congregation typically sings a total of four songs. The service begins with the singing of verses 4 and, sometimes, 5 of the hymn "He's Taking a Wife" (*Ausbund* 69).

> (*verse 4*) *He has taken a wife,*
> *The Christian Church in the Spirit,*
> *Love has compelled Him,*
> *Which He also has shown to us.*
> *His life He has set before us,*
> *Those who also likewise love Him*
> *Are also chosen unto Him.*

As in other worship services, the second song on the roster is the *Loblied*. Along with the local ministers, all the ministers related to the family of the bride and groom who have come from near and far for the wedding find a private space to instruct the bride and groom during the first two songs. The local leaders have met with the couple prior to the wedding, so they allow the visiting ministers to take the lead. The couple hears multiple perspectives about the meaning and responsibilities of marriage.

When the couple and the ministers return from the *Abrot*, the congregants sing the fourth verse of the *Ausbund* hymn 378 (see appendix I, Musical Example A1.10). This slow song, written around 1540 by Siegmund von Bosch, prefigures the wedding of Jesus Christ with the faithful church as predicted in the Bible.[1]

The local bishop preaches the first sermon, on the theme of the need for the new husband to be a Christian leader. Otherwise, how can his wife follow him? This sermon instructs the whole congregation, reconfirming the values and norms of the group. The congregation kneels, and another minister offers a prayer. A third minister reads the scriptures for weddings, Ephesians 5:21–33 and 1 Corinthians 7:1–9, and another sermon follows. As in other services, each preacher seeks a witness. A visiting preacher expresses what the particular passage of Scripture means to him.

The ministers stand alongside the couple and read the marriage vows. Among the questions they ask is: "Do you also have the confidence, brother (sister), that the Lord has ordained this our fellow sister (brother) to be your wedded wife (husband)? The couple answers, "Yes."[2]

The gathering sings "Ermuntert euch, ihr frommen" to the tune of "Bind Us Together." Then they sing "Ich will lieben" to the tune of "The Battle Hymn of the Republic" (a camp meeting song borrowed earlier for "John Brown's Body") or "The Marine Hymn" (a tune from an opera by Jacques Offenbach). It seems that despite their pacifist background, the Amish have decided that these tunes transcend their wartime history. A blessing prayer ensues. The final hymn, "Gelobt sei Gott," (*Ausbund* 712), "Praise be God in the highest throne, / Who clothed us with a beautiful coat, / So we are born anew. / This is the true wedding garment," completes the service (see appendix I, Musical Example A1.11).

Following the service, a reception meal takes place at the bride's home. The large crowd of guests, which can number up to eight hundred people, can rarely be accommodated at one sitting. Families attempt to restrict the number invited, but they may not be successful. Large coolers powered by gas generators keep massive quantities of food cold and fresh. For the Old Order Amish who refuse to use generators, many weddings occur in winter. In the past, the family also served an evening supper, and the youth stayed around for a midnight meal. With the increased numbers at weddings, a family can only manage serving one meal.

After lunch, the older folks start singing. They open with the last hymn of the service, "A Wedding Hymn," followed by the third song of the service, "Er hat ein Weis genommen." The song leaders of the district take turns choosing the other songs. In the meantime, young married couples reset the tables and serve lunch to the young folks. For an hour or so, the group sings *Ausbund* songs that give advice about building a Christian marriage through prayer, reading the Bible, and, not surprisingly, singing together. The group may harmonize on songs from the *Liedersammlung* and other favorite gospel hymnals. In good weather, the young people may follow up the singing with a volleyball game.

Between the pre-service singing, the singing in the service itself, and the post-lunch singing, the wedding day has been filled as much with music as with almost any other element. Prayer for and admonition to the bride and groom have been offered, of course, as well as lots of conversation and food. Music has threaded throughout the day's events, adding colorful reminders of the couple's history, community, and commitments.

Much like weddings, funerals function as a worship service that draws friends and family from miles, even states away. Singing often wends its way through the day of an Amish funeral, although to a lesser degree than at a wedding. For funerals, music provides relief and support for the mourners. Songs chosen for funerals give solace to the survivors but also allow all the other attendees to review *their* lives and to assess how close they are to God.

Music for Funerals

> Come, children, let us go, the evening draws near;
> It is dangerous to stand in this wilderness.
> Come, strengthen your courage to wander on to eternity,
> From one power to the other the end is good.
> We shall not regret the narrow pilgrim path,
> For we know the faithful One who has called us.
> Come, follow and trust God, each one turn around completely,
> And face directly and firmly toward Jerusalem.[3]

The line of black buggies presents a somber scene as the family rides to the cemetery for the burial of their forty-five-year-old mother who fell victim to cancer. The body is laid to rest in a simple casket after group prayers. All sing the songs her children have chosen for the service, songs that will comfort and assure them of seeing their beloved mother again (see appendix I, Musical Example A1.12).

On the morning of the funeral, the immediate family assembles by eight o'clock. The ministers lead a short, private service. After this, the family moves to the main gathering in a workshop, barn, or house where friends await. By about nine o'clock, the first minister begins preaching for a half hour. The second minister adds another fifteen to twenty minutes of comfort and exhortation, to assure that those present are themselves ready to meet God. Then, the bishop takes over. He preaches for a full thirty to forty-five minutes. The main purposes of each of these messages include interpreting the rules of a godly life, urging members to follow the instructions, and eulogizing the deceased. Sometimes ministers remind congregants that no one can say for certain that the deceased has gone to heaven. "God alone will judge the life and belief of the deceased, but the faithful can have hope," one bishop explains. Some New Order groups believe that the saved can have an assurance of salvation as long as they stay faithful. The bishop closes with a prayer and a benediction.

Depending on which Amish group is holding the funeral, there may or may not be singing during the funeral or graveside service. Pennsylvanian Frederick Klees wrote about an Amish funeral service he attended in 1961 during which the Amish sang no songs.[4] Many Old Order and other stricter Amish groups only read a hymn at the graveside. While music offers solace, the Old Order Amish simply say, "This is not our way." Perhaps, singing seems too frivolous for the somber occasion. Songs read at Old Order funerals in Pennsylvania include verses from *Ausbund* hymns 357, 358, 390, and 437 and texts from the *Liedersammlung* 173, "Ach! Was ist doch unter Leb'n?" "Alle Menschen müssen Sterben," "Nun gute Nacht, ihr Liebsten mein," "Freu dich sehr, O meine Seele," "Mein Lebensfaden lauft zu Ende," "On Jordan's Stormy Banks I Stand," or "Herzlich tut mich verlangen"[5]:

> Herzlich tut mich verlangen
> Nach einem sel'gen End,
> Weil ich bin hier umsangen
> Mit Trübsal und Elend;
> Ich hab Lust abzuscheiden
> Von dieser bösen Welt,

Sehn mich nach ew'gen Freuden,
Sonst nichts mir hier gesällt.

Sincerely I desire
After a blessed end
Because I am surrounded
With sorrow and distress;
I desire to part
From this evil world,
Yearning after eternal joy,
Moreover nothing here pleases me.[6]

In Holmes County, some Old and New Order Amish have chosen to sing at funerals because they recognize the comfort they receive from their favorite hymns. In New Order funeral services, the congregants sing "Gott ist die Liebe," the *Lobsang*, and "Nun sich der Tag" ("When the Day Has Ended")[7]:

Nun sich der Tag geendet hat,
Und keine Sonn mehr scheint,
Ruht alles, was sich abgematt't,
Und was zuvor geweint.
Nur du den Schlaf nicht nöthig hast,
Mein Gott! Du schlummerst nicht;
Die Finsterniss ist dir verhasst,
Weil du bist selbst das Licht.

When the day has ended,
And the sun no longer shines.
Everything that becomes faint
And has wept will rest.
Only God needs no sleep.
My God, You never slumber.
The darkness You have hated
Because You are Light itself.

They might also sing "Wer weiss" ("Who Knows What My End Shall Be"):

Wer weiss, wie nahe mir mein Ende?
Die Zeit geht him, es kommt der Tod;
Ach, wie geschwinde und behende
Kann kommen meine Todesnoth.
Mein Gott! Ich bitt durch Christi Blut,
Mach's nur mit meinem Ende gut.

Who knows, how near is my end?
The time passes and death comes;
Oh, how swiftly and quickly
Can come death's distress,
My God, I pray through Christ's blood
To make my end good.

If the deceased still has children at home, the congregation may sing "Kommt Kinder, lasst uns gehen" ("Come, Children, Let Us Go"). "Kommt Kinder" relates a caution from a parent to her or his children as to how difficult it is to remain true to God in this evil world. "Follow me towards eternity," the deceased beckons.

At the graveside service of a New Order group, after everyone sings one song, the youth walk by the casket first, then they stand to one side and softly sing four or five songs, such as "Wo ist Jesus mein Verlangen" or "Es sind zween Weg." The rest of the assembly files by the coffin to say goodbye. Just before the family goes to the coffin, a minister reads a psalm.

Burial practices also vary from one area to another. For example, in Middlefield, Ohio, the Amish have an open casket for the viewing of the body, which is rare in Holmes County. In Holmes County, everyone, children and all, follows the coffin to the grave. Reading of Scripture and singing may continue at the graveside. At one funeral, the bishop and group alternate; the bishop reads two lines and the group sings two lines of "Gute Nacht ihr meine Lieben."[8] Most Amish sing the same tune used for "Schaffet, Schaffet, meine Kinder" (see appendix I, Musical Example A1.7), but the Holmes County Amish use their own tune (Musical Example 11.1). "Our tune is more mournful," a woman explains.[9] After eight phrases of call and response, the bishop continues to read the hymn text.

Some groups sing songs in English at the graveside. Songs for the loss of a mother abound, including: "Meet Mother in the Skies," "Mother's Grave," "Mother Left Me Her Bible," and a song asking, "If my mother

Musical Example 11.1. "Schaffet, Schaffet, meine Kinder" / "Gute Nacht ihr meine
Lieben," Holmes County (2008).
Gute Nacht, ihr meine Kinder (Lieben);
Gute Nacht, ihr Herzensfreund;
Gute Nacht die sich betrüben,
Und aus Lieb für mich jetst weint.
Sheid' ich gleichwohl von euch ab,
Und ihr legt mein Leib ins Grab,
Wird er wieder auferstehen,
Und ich werd euch ewig sehen.
Translation: *Good night, my child (loved one);*
Good night, my bosom friends;
Good night, you who grieve,
And out of love now weep for me.
Even though I part from you,
And you lay my body in the grave,
It shall rise again,
And I will see you eternally.

had not prayed for me—where would I be?" (see appendix I, Musical Example A1.13).

At the funeral for a child, the Amish often sing "Ich war ein kleines
Kindlein." One Amish man says that people in his area were unfamil-
iar with the tune, so he often sang it alone at funerals. Today, more have
learned it. He sings the song with embellishments that are not notated
in Troyer's Ausbund *and* Liedersammlung *Songs* (1997). For example, he
precedes many of the pairs of notes with the second of the two as an anticipation to the main note (Musical Example 11.2). For example, the music

for the syllable "Ich" is written B to G, but he sings it G to B to G. Likewise, "war" is A to G but sung G to A to G.

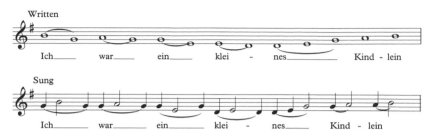

Musical Example 11.2. First phrase of "Ich war ein kleines Kindlein."
Sources: Troyer, Ausbund *and* Liedersammlung *Songs*, 78. Atlee Miller, personal interview, Feb. 2007.
Translation: *I was a small child born into this world;*
As to my time of death
I have nothing to say what goes on in the earth;
I have built, created nothing in my time on earth.

An aunt reveals that her sixteen-year-old nephew died within two
months of a cancer diagnosis. His family chose "How Beautiful Heaven
Must Be" for graveside singing. Family members filed by the grave, placed
a shovelful of dirt on the casket, a tradition taking hold in Holmes County,
and sang:

> *We read of a place that's called heaven,*
> *It's made for the pure and the free;*
> *These truths in God's Word He hath given,*
> *How beautiful heaven must be.*
> *How beautiful heaven must be,*
> *Sweet home of the happy and free,*
> *Fair haven of rest for the weary,*
> *How beautiful heaven must be.*[10]

Throughout the cycle of life, a typical Amish person is immersed in
corporate worship. For ceremonies such as weddings and funerals, which
mark the passage of time, the Amish choose songs that reflect the grav-
ity and tenor of the occasion. We turn now to the songs that accompany
Amish people through their more typical activities—the songs they sing
as they work, celebrate holidays, travel, and perform the various tasks of
daily life.

CHAPTER 12

Songs of Trust
Music in Daily Life

Wer weiß, wie nahe mir mein Ende?	*Who knows how near is my end?*
Die Zeit geht hin, es kommt der Tod;	*Time goes by, and death draws near,*
Ach wie geschwinde und behende	*Oh, how promptly and quickly*
Kann kommen meine Todesnot.	*Can come the peril of death.*
Mein Gott! Ich bitt durch Christi Blut,	*My God, I plead through Christ's blood,*
Machs nur mit meinem Ende gut.	*Grant only that my end be good!*

—*Ausbund* (1564/1997)

J udy and I sit at her family's kitchen table while her mother finishes drying the dinner dishes. The modern kitchen has polished wooden cupboards, linoleum that wraps around the corner to the front door, and gas filament lamps. Judy disappears into another room and soon returns with a stack of songbooks. "Some of my friends wanted to learn to read [musical] notes, so the girls came for lessons," she tells me. "But now that I'm teaching fulltime, I don't have time."

Judy comes from a musical family. "We used to sing a lot before my older brother and sister got married," she tells me. "We don't do that too often now. My father writes songs. He is a bleeder [hemophiliac]. When he gets sick and has to stay in bed, he writes songs, both the music and the words."

Judy's voice holds an uncharacteristic note of pride as she tells me that two of her father's songs have actually been published. She smiles, turns to one of his hymns in a hymnal from the stack she has retrieved, and sings:

When I'm facing sorest trials, and the pain is hard to bear,
I will not be discontented, nor will sing in dark despair;

For I know He has a purpose, and I trust in Him alone,
May the outcome of affliction prove to be a stepping stone.
Chorus: Stepping stones to Gloryland, God will place them on our way;
Step by step, we dare not falter, He'll direct our steps each day.
Satan tries to make us stumble, our endeavors he will mock;
But our trust will be in Jesus, safe upon the solid Rock.[1]

Singing has played an important role in Judy's family. Even as the amount of singing they do together has ebbed and flowed, it has remained a formative force in their communal life. For Judy's father, singing serves as a way to survive, a strategy to cope with his difficult health condition. It helps him to reach a place of trust in divine providence, as the lyrics of his song indicate.

All songs that the Amish sing could be considered "songs of trust," of course, not just the songs that we examine in this chapter. Trust in God plays a central role in Amish theology and practice. Yielding to the will of God is a belief and habit that the practice of singing helps Amish people develop. In this chapter, we look at a miscellany of singing events in Amish lives. The variety of singing scenarios described in this chapter adds credence to the claim that singing serves a vital role in the sustenance of Amish identity and culture.

Shut-Ins

Ministers and caring church members often gather around the sickbeds of loved ones to offer solace, and music is often a part of this caregiving practice. They sing songs such as "Wer weiss, wie nahe" and "The World Is Not My home" (see appendix I, Musical Example A1.14):

> The world is not my home,
> I'm just a-passing through,
> My treasures are laid up
> Somewhere beyond the blue;
> The angels beckon me
> From heaven's open door,
> And I can't feel at home
> In this world anymore.

One woman offered that a group of her friends rent a van once a month to visit with three or four shut-in friends for talking and singing.

Singing to the Horses

Many Amish report singing to pass the time or to encourage themselves when they are working. One woman tells me about a song she sings while sweeping, in which she thanks God for the blessings of shelter and health. "I like to hear singing but don't sing much since my wife died," reports one older Amish man, and then adds: "Oh, I do still sing to the horses in the field."[2]

Sisters preserve fruits and vegetables, talk, laugh, and sing hymns in harmony. "This tune is very old. We have sung it for many, many years," an Old Order woman tells me; "When I feel good, I sing or whistle while I work. We also sing as a family when everyone's here, like at Christmas." Katie offers "Wo ist Jesus mein Verlangen" ("Where Is Jesus, My Desire") as one of her favorites to sing while she works (see appendix I, Musical Example A1.15). She sings the notes evenly, with no dotted notes:

> Where is Jesus, my Desire,
> My beloved Lord and Friend,
> Where is he then gone?
> Where may I find him?
> My soul is very distressed
> With many sins languishing;
> Where is Jesus whom I love
> The one I desire day and night?

Women gather for monthly quiltings, where they place even, white stitches in a quilt—or perhaps two, if there are enough women to spread out. In the past, they sent the finished quilts to missions overseas. Now, so many relief sales are held in the area that they frequently donate the quilts for auction, with the proceeds going to things such as school funds or mission projects in Haiti. Talking and singing accompany quilting sessions. Singing maintains the pace, eases the potential tedium of repetitive activities, and reconnects singers to pleasant events.

Older men get together to practice with younger men to help them develop as *Vorsingers*. "Single girls"—unmarried women in their late twenties and older—meet to make greeting cards, to sew, and to enjoy each other's company. These casual events are always occasions for singing, to add to the pleasure of being together.

Holy Days, Holy Songs

Holidays include family gatherings enhanced by particular songs. For Christmas, the children open their presents, which are usually a few toys. Some families exchange names so that even the adults receive a present. One family requires that all presents be homemade. The group attends a service on Christmas Day, where they will undoubtedly sing "Von Himmel hoch da" (see appendix I, Musical Example A1.16)[3]:

> *From heaven on high I come here*
> *To bring you good tiding of salvation and grace*
> *This good news I bring so abundantly*
> *Of which I wish to tell in song.*
> *Unto you this day a Child is born,*
> *From a certain virgin chosen [of God],*
> *A Child, so tender and fine,*
> *Shall be your joy and delight.*[4]

The worship services take the same form as usual. No decorations grace the meeting area, although one woman said she carries a poinsettia-decorated handkerchief to Christmas services. Simplicity remains the rule, the focus of worship praise of God for God's goodness. The meal after worship is the usual family fare.

Major holy days such as Christmas and Easter present another good time to visit widows and homebound members. At Easter, a youth group encircles a minister's home early in the morning to awaken him with singing. Some families celebrate Easter by coloring eggs. At Thanksgiving, another youth group fixes Thanksgiving plates or takes boxes of groceries to those they visit.

At New Year's, friends and family gather informally. The hosts serve sauerkraut, sausage, and mashed potatoes. "Every year we ask each other, 'Why don't we eat this more often? It tastes so good,'" reports one woman. "We do like to get together to fellowship and talk."[5] Amish services include the song "Heut sänget" at the beginning of the new year; one man sings the often-used "fast" tune (see appendix I, Musical Example A1.17), then he recalls singing another tune as a child decades ago. He tries out a few melodies before he settles on one. He evinces no embarrassment as he works out tunes or even when he gives up and quits.

Amish birthdays are simple celebrations. One Amish mother said she and her husband gave her little boy a yo-yo, a pair of sandals, and a pillow for his fifth birthday.[6] Decade birthdays receive more attention in some Amish groups. For a fortieth, or "black fortieth," age mates who have been lifelong friends bring black balloons and serenade the birthday celebrant awake. For other milestone birthdays, the guests bring finger foods, visit, and sing.

"My Heart Remains with You"

At the end of gatherings with friends, the Amish sometimes employ a goodnight or goodbye song, especially for visitors who have come from long distances. The lyrics of one song request God's protection and guidance, and the singer employs another "fast" tune, "Just as I Am," with additional 'cuts' or escape tones (see appendix I, Musical Example A1.18). Another melody for the same text uses a "slow" tune that emphasizes the second note in each pair of notes by holding it longer, as in the parting hymn "Lebt friedsam" (Live peaceably) (see appendix I, Musical Example A1.19). In "Lebt friedsam," the penultimate line of each stanza refers to the blessings of being together that are celebrated at the time of parting:

> Live peacefully, said Christ the Lord,
> To His chosen ones,
> Beloved, take this for a teaching,
> And gladly listen for His voice.
> This is said in parting from me
> That you would firmly stand,
> Even though I leave my heart remains with you
> Till we enter into joy.

Another parting song contains a melismatic melody with four or more notes on most syllables (see appendix I, Musical Example A1.20). Of these four parting songs, three are hexatonic, using six of the seven notes of the scale. The fourth note of the modal scale is missing in "Nun Gott lob!," the seventh in both "Lebt friedsam" and "Weil nun der Zeit."

Singing the Journey

Early in the morning, an Amish bishop and all his siblings and their spouses pile into a fifteen-passenger van for a five-hour drive to an Amish community in western New York. "Four families have gone to start a new community," his wife explains to me. "We'll help them have a worship service. They do not have a minister yet. The van ride is as much fun as the annual reunion. We can catch up on everyone's family business and sing. It's very lively."[7]

A van may take a group of Amish shopping, to a funeral or wedding, or to visit a sick friend or family members. The riders divide the cost of the trip—van, gas, and driver—by the number of people on board. Trips may take the Amish to visit relatives who have moved to other states (with some New Order Amish taking plane rides if their children are living in other countries) or to help a new settlement needing additional ministers or members to hold their biannual communion. Some trips are relaxing vacations; others, whirlwind trips. One Amish woman tells me that she has been to Niagara Falls five or six times.

A favorite excursion for the Amish in Ohio is a trip to Lancaster, Pennsylvania, to enjoy a Bible play. The Green Country Tour, led by David and Irene Swartzentruber, takes groups to see the year's dramas, which could be "Abraham and Judy: A Journey of Love," "Daniel: A Dream, a Den, a Deliverer," "Noah, the Musical," "Ruth," or "The Miracle of Christmas." These magical shows feature live animals such as chickens and white horses as part of the performance. Leaving early in the morning and driving six or so hours east on Interstate 30, the tour offers a doubleheader of plays at the Sight & Sound Theatres, an overnight in a budget motel, and a guided tour of the Kreider dairy farm, with the largest milking parlor in the East. The group then returns to the Ohio settlement the next day.

The forty-passenger bus, at seventy-five dollars per person (including play tickets but not meals), fills to capacity. Luggage stowed, the people settle in their seats. The tour guide says a prayer in Pennsylvania Dutch for traveling protection and asks that God be honored in their encounters. The tour guide passes out songbooks printed especially for the bus ride. The guide is a cheerleader and jokester, starting a song and then holding the microphone up to one person after another for karaoke-style solos. Much laughter greets the performer.

"I like to sing with a group, but I don't like to lead or sing solos," confides one woman. She continues, "We stress that you have to think about the words that you are singing. We are praising God. We realize that."[8] They sing several songs, people calling out the numbers of their favorites. They sing the *Loblied*, the familiar *Ausbund* praise song, but they use the tune of William Bradbury's "Sweet Hour of Prayer" in 3/4 time.[9]

Other favorites include "The Family Who Prays," "I'll Fly Away," "This Is My Story," and "Jesus Signed My Pardon," which reaffirms that the work of Jesus frees the repentant from fear of judgment. A singer tries out the song and needs a second take to get the melody right. The tour group takes a break from singing, and conversation becomes general. The bus stops once during the journey for leg-stretching and a sit-down restaurant meal. As the bus pulls out, the singing and talking alternate.

Some tours offer travel to the western United States, even Alaska, or east to New York City. The Amish travelers do not go to Broadway shows, but they might visit Ground Zero, the New York Stock Exchange, and the Empire State Building. One New Order man speaks of his pilgrimage to Münster, Germany, to see the place where Anabaptists were burned out of their village and murdered as they tried to escape.

Singing for shut-ins, while working, at holidays, to say goodbye, and while traveling are just some of the many contexts in which music happens among the Amish. Because pastimes remain limited, singing will continue to hold an important, even central, position. The *Vorsingers*, hymn translators, young people, and others in the Amish community with greater interest in the whys and hows of singing will have their influence on their friends. And singing, an unsung hero, will continue to flourish and enliven the community.

CHAPTER 13

Songs for the Future
Amish Singing in the Twenty-First Century

Christus das Lamm auf Erden kam,	*Christ the Lamb came upon earth,*
Nach's Vaters Rath und Willen,	*According to the counsel and will of the Father,*
Alles was Gott verheissen hat,	*All that God has promised,*
Dasselb thut er erfüllen,	*This He does fulfill,*
Wie Adams Schuld, uns die Unhuld	*Just as Adam's transgression brought us*
Bracht, und göttlichen Zoren,	*Disfavor and God's wrath,*
Dasselbig ist, durch Jesum Christ	*This, through Jesus Christ,*
Wieder versöhnet worden.	*Is reconciled again.*

—Ausbund (1564/1997)

I t's a good thing we didn't know how bad he was," whispers the bishop's wife as she describes her husband's terrible condition after an automobile rammed his buggy from behind. The impact threw him through the buggy's roof onto the road. His horse broke loose and ran to safety in a field. The bishop's body was so broken that two hospitals turned him away before the squad found one where the doctors thought they could help him. "They let him lie still for a full week, not even cleaning the dirt and leaves from his skin and clothes for fear of doing more damage," his wife continues.

The bishop was in so much pain that he couldn't sleep and prayed for release. Friends and family took turns calling him on the phone and singing him to sleep. The old songs he had been hearing from the time he was a child offered deep solace as he lay in bed for what seemed like countless hours. Whether singing prevented the bishop's death remains unproven, of course; what is known is that the singing support of his community accompanied him through an unexpected and remarkable recovery. Four months later, he was walking again and returned to work and worship.

The bishop's experience of being sung through suffering and into survival can serve as a metaphor for the role of music among Amish people throughout the centuries. The Amish sing for their survival. John Blacking warns, in "*A Commonsense View of All Music*": *Reflections on Percy Grainger's Contribution to Ethnomusicology and Music Education*, that a society's culture is fleeting and "survives only as long as people use it. A culture is always being invented and reinvented by individual decision-making."[1] Singing is a daily act of renewing, invigorating, and even reinventing the culture that has formed them and that now forms their children. The Amish sing old songs in the old way and also in new ways—with "vocal vagaries," as musicologist George Pullen Jackson calls the characteristic waverings of Amish music—with newer melodies, and with harmony to add musical interest and community delight. They adjust their singing, like other aspects of their culture, to meet the demands of living in a postmodern world. The adaptability of music itself becomes a resource that helps the Amish to survive as cultures collide. In this final chapter, we look at Amish singing as a strategy for managing change and also at the ways it may continue to evolve in the future.

Music as a Window on Change

Singing provides a powerful way for outsiders to access and understand the adaptations occurring within a culture, adaptations that otherwise may be invisible. Historian Lawrence W. Levine explains, "Culture is not a fixed condition but a process: the product of interaction between the past and present. Its toughness and resiliency are determined not by a culture's ability to withstand change, which indeed may be a sign of stagnation not life, but by its ability to react creatively and responsively to the realities of a new situation."[2] Consequently, singing provides a critical form of resistance, helping the community to choose, adjust, and adapt while preserving some traditions from the incursions of the modern world. Observing Amish singing events opens a window into their changing worldview and changing practices. Let's examine several of these changes in more detail.

The first notable change in Amish singing habits, at least in Ohio, is, in fact, a change that actually heightens tradition. Among the Amish in

Wayne and Holmes Counties, there appears to be a renaissance of *Ausbund* singing. Men are meeting to practice the worship songs to be able to lead them more securely. "Our group noticed that we needed men's singing rehearsals to develop the singing in worship and maintain the old tunes of the *Ausbund*," bishop Jacob Beachy reflects. To address this need, they meet during the winter months, when work demands are lighter. Elders are delighted that many young men decided to join them and that they are developing a proficiency in singing the slow songs, taking their turns leading in worship. Also, with the advent of Wednesday night Bible studies in the New Order community, some youth groups gather to sing twice a week. Both Old Order and New Order Amish report that, in their assessment, worship singing is improving.

Singing in parts is another change that has become more common among the Amish, particularly among the New Order. But, as mentioned in chapter 2, part-singing is only sanctioned at informal gatherings. Mennonites, close ecclesial cousins to the Amish, often sing in four-part harmony, and musical cross-fertilization between the two does occur. Amish interviewees commonly express the "official" position that their people sing in unison, but when asked directly if or when they sing in parts, some verbalize that monophonic singing is preferred but that their youth do sing in parts. Of course, the adults meet with the youth at "youth sings," and all sing. But adults rarely admit that they, too, sing in parts. At one Christmas gathering of a public school that serves only Amish pupils, scholars and their relatives sing "Stille Nacht" in heavenly, four-part harmony with Mennonite teachers and English guests. For all, because the *Ausbund* hymns stand in a position of centrality, monophony remains the preferred texture in singing, even though part-singing is no longer taboo for informal gatherings in many communities.

The proliferation of melodies is another notable change in Amish singing life. "When we were younger, we didn't branch out; we just used a basic set of tunes," says Atlee Miller, a youthful eighty-year-old *Vorsinger* and grandfather of forty-three. Now there are so many!" Atlee recalls the songs from his childhood and re-teaches the old tunes to Amish family and friends in Pennsylvania, Iowa, Kentucky, and parts of Ohio. In this way, he hopes to recover and revitalize the tradition of the old songs. Atlee's singing style includes a confident, in-tune singing voice, many anticipations, a light slurring between pitches, and a slow, steady speed. Along with spreading the old tunes of the martyr songs, Atlee is keeping the old singing style alive while also enjoying the new melodies. He is one of the older *Vorsingers* who seek to maintain, even revive, the old tunes, thereby serving as a cultural buffer negotiating both change and continuity. When Atlee's friends sing with him, they constantly gush, "This tune is beautiful and enjoyable."

As tunes have proliferated, texts have changed. Early Anabaptist hymns specifically urge singers to praise God and admonish them to live as disciples no matter the personal cost. But in times when persecution abates, the need for cross-bearing and martyrdom moves to the background.[3] More recent songs teach Amish vocalists to stay true when life is easy and materialism lures seductively. The Amish have continually chosen to sing the hymns that praise and promote reliance on God, of course, from early *Ausbund* hymns to carefully selected gospel hymns. But changes are afoot in the textual content of Amish songs; occasionally even patriotic folksongs such as "This Land Is Your Land" are included in Amish informal singing repertoires.

An example of these textual changes can be found in the singing of the familiar Christian Sunday school song "Jesus Loves Me," which represents an emphasis on a personal relationship with God and an evangelical thrust that has been increasing in strength among many Amish people. While we don't know the frequency with which "Jesus Loves Me" was sung among Amish people in previous generations, we do know that it is now the first song that many Amish children learn to sing, and they frequently sing it in school. Also, most Amish adults cite it as one of their favorites.

The evangelical turn in some Amish communities is evidenced in their choice of songs and articulation of their meaning. Lifestyle is not the important factor for many Amish. It is their relationship with God and, by extension, the community. One thirty-year-old Amish mother confides, "The words are very meaningful. When you're young, you just sing it; but as you get older, you have a fuller understanding of the meaning of how Jesus loves you." An Amish woman in her forties explains, "It is a comforting thought that there is somebody heavenly that loves me and cares about me. It is also comforting [for children] if they ever become scared. Singing 'Jesus Loves Me' gives parents the opportunity to tell children about Jesus and teach them, in times of trouble, you can always look to Jesus." "Jesus helps us to feel safe in His love," reveals another. And a sixty-eight-year-old Amish man urges, "Jesus loves us first so we owe him love too. He loved us first when he let himself be crucified. We now owe him love in return."[4]

The more things change, certainly, the more they stay the same. Even as these changes are occurring, many aspects of Amish singing life remain constant. Melismatic chant from the *Ausbund* remains primary, even as newer tunes and texts make their way into Amish repertoires. Women's role in singing also offers a bellwether of continuity. Just as Amish gender roles remain traditional, with husbands retaining the decision-making responsibility and ordained men leading ecclesiastical life, accordingly song leading in worship basically remains the purview of Amish men. Girls and women lead singing at youth hymn sings and in other informal settings, such as at a New Year's gathering. Men's roles as leaders in all things spiritual extend to singing as a spiritual tool.

And it is not presumptuous to claim that, following another tradition, Amish singing will remain solidly participatory and congregational well into the future. Unlike the music of many other churches, which regularly include performances or selections by choirs or worship teams or individuals, Amish music remains an expression of community life. As such, it includes everyone, not just a few, in its production. Regardless of musical ability or vocal quality, everyone participates. Amish singing thus provides a way of cooperating and supporting the community.

Singing for Survival

The Amish truly sing for their survival. In worship, all sing in unison the songs written by martyrs who would not bow to the pressures of the state demanding that they recant and conform to the world. They sing slowly and ponder the texts, which present appropriate ways of teaching children, seeking God in the silence and praising in all circumstances, above all in days of want and persecution. The old hymns link the group to generations of Amish people, soothing and guiding the singers.

Amish singing teaches the singers to give God praise, as in "In der stillen Einsamkeit" and "Gelobt sei Gott im hochsten Thron"; to prepare themselves as though death were imminent, as in "Bedenke Mensch, das Ende"; to strive for humility, as in "Demuth ist die schönste Tugend"; and to live as peacemakers, as in "Lebt friedsam." Singing provides the Amish with a source of community solidarity, a testimony to godliness, and a means of resistance. Praising God simply, with the voice, without instrumental accompaniment and without embellishment, reinforces the purity of Amish worship and forms a counterpoint to their desire to live in God's will.

Singing toward Selflessness

A story that emerged from the Nickel Mines Amish school shooting in Pennsylvania on October 2, 2006, brings us full circle to the first song, "Bedenke Mensch, das Ende," that we examined in chapter 1. It also poignantly underscores the central role of singing in Amish life, the way it carries memory, identity, devotion, and culture from one generation to another.

The killing of five Amish girls and the injuring of several others by a gunman in a murder-suicide horrified the world and brought much attention to the Amish way of life. Media stories quickly turned to the actions of the Amish in the wake of the shooting. Stunning to outsiders was the fact that the Amish reached out to the shooter's family, visiting and bringing gifts of food and attending the gunman's funeral.

Remarkable, too, were the words and actions of one of the Amish girls before she was killed. Thirteen-year-old Marian Fisher rapidly became a leader of the group being held hostage and tried to protect the younger girls from the gunman. At one point, according to children who escaped, Marian said to the intruder as he held the children at gunpoint: "Shoot me first, and let the others go."

The moral integrity of a child who, in the face of mortal danger, pleads on behalf of others rather than herself is incredible and, indeed, beyond words. Lesser-known than Marian's words, however, is the fact that that very morning, before the shooter entered the schoolhouse, Marian and her classmates had sung the classic Amish hymn, "Bedenke Mensch, das Ende" ("Consider, Human, the End"), which the children sang during many of my visits to Amish schools (see table 6.1).[5] To the tune of "Bind Us Together with Love," the children in the Nickel Mines schoolhouse had sung these words in German:

> Consider, human, the end,
> Consider your death.
> Death often comes quickly.
> Today you are healthy and ruddy,

Tomorrow and even sooner,
You poor wretch, are suddenly dead;
Every day, sinner,
Imagine yourself as dying.[6]

The tragic ending of the story—that Marian and four of her classmates died, and five others sustained serious injuries—may suggest that singing and survival are sometimes cruelly disconnected. It is true that Marian and her four friends did not survive. Yet the virtues of forgiveness, community, and compassion that explicitly imbue their favorite songs did. Singing songs such as "Bedenke Mensch, das Ende" was one of the many practices of humility and self-denial that had formed young Marian Fisher and prepared her for heroism. Was it possible that the songs of the martyrs and other hymns shaped Marian's identity to the extent that she was willing to offer herself in place of her friends? "The stories and songs of the faith that she had learned will certainly be passed down to generations after hers," write the authors of *Amish Grace*. "The song she and her classmates had sung that morning will carry a sad and profound resonance for years to come."[7]

Singing their way through suffering, the Amish have long been accustomed to the ways in which music accompanies individuals and cultures through dark days. Singing not only preserves an Amish identity but enlivens and enlarges it, helping the community respond to change with both flexibility and continuity. Their songs of survival serve as a witness both to the precariousness and the buoyancy of the Amish culture. From their long-used hymnal, the *Ausbund*, they sing:

Teach your children clearly God's word and commandment,
Then let God work. This is a fine treasure.
If you live according to what you teach the children,
You, then, give a good example through which God is praised.[8]

Additional Musical Examples

This appendix offers a few more musical examples with a short discussion of some, along with some comparisons to other musical examples.

Musical Example A1.1. "Es sind zween Weg," Library of Congress (1941).
Source: Frey, "Hymns as Folk Music," 155.

In his article "Amish Hymns as Folk Music," J. William Frey includes the version shown in Musical Example A1.1, which closely follows the transcription in Yoder's 1942 *Amische Lieder*. For example, in the first line, the sole change is that Frey's Library of Congress version has a short quarter note (one beat) on the last note of the phrase, compared with a double whole note (eight beats) in the Yoder. It is likely that these two hymn collectors knew the same source. However, the next two examples each employed a second tune that differs markedly from the one that Frey and Yoder used.

In 1997, Amishman Ben Troyer, Jr., published a volume called Ausbund *and* Liedersammlung *Songs*, which includes sixty-nine texts and melodies. Comparing the FAR version in Musical Example A1.2 to the one in Troyer's book (Musical Example A1.3), they both have the same order of pitches, but Troyer uses identical note values for each note in the tune. If an untrained singer tried to sing the song, she wouldn't know the rhythm and would be forced to sing all the notes as the same length—or ad lib as she desired. The Troyer version includes four notes on the third syllable "zween" rather than two, as in the FAR version. The FAR version includes

an extra note on "die-ser." Also, the second and third lines of the Troyer are dupli-
cates until the second to the last syllable. Specifically, the second line ends F-E-F-F
and the third line, F-E-C-C-E. In the FAR version, the singers sing the second line
but use the third line of text ending the line as in the Troyer third line. This confuses
them. They go on to the fourth and final line of the Troyer melody with the text of
the third line and end it awkwardly (Musical Example A1.3).

Musical Example A1.2. "Es sind zween Weg," Former Amish Reunion (2001).

Musical Example A1.3. "Es sind zween Weg," Modern Notation of Troyer (1997).

Just as in poetry where a poet writes in iambic, short-long, or trochee, long-short,
or dactyl, long-short-short, a particular rhythmic pattern is used throughout a song.
In the FAR version (Musical Example A1.1), a preponderance of short-long pair-
ings for each syllable of text hints at twelfth-century modal notation.

Another way to consider differences is to compare the melodic cadences, the
approaches to the final note, of each melodic line of thirteen melodies from Yoder's
Amische Lieder and thirteen melodies from Troyer's edition; this comparison reveals
some striking dissimilarities (table A1.1). Since different Amish communities produced each version, it becomes obvious that regional variations exist. The span of
notes that fit comfortably in general group singing ranges from the smallest of a major sixth to the largest of an octave and a fourth in the Troyer edition and an octave
and a fifth in the Yoder edition. While both use the shape note tradition, Yoder

Table A1.1 Comparison of cadences of Troyer and Yoder versions

	Troyer's Ausbund and Liedersammlung Songs		Yoder's Amische Lieder	
Upper neighbor tone, anticipation, final	71	70.3%	40	51.9%
Upper neighbor, lower neighbor, final	19	18.8%	4	5.2%
Final, upper neighbor, final	1	1.0%	20	25.9%
Descending notes to final	0	0	5	6.5%
Other	10	10.0%	8	10.3%
Total cadences	101		77	

gives specific pitches for his songs, while Troyer only provides the notes in relation to each other. Therefore, *do* could be any pitch that sits comfortably in the congregational voice range.

The FAR and the Troyer versions of "Es sind zween Weg" are sung slowly, at quarter note = 69. The melodies of both are neumatic, with two to three (and occasionally four) notes per syllable of text. Only four syllables, one of which is the final, have but one note, and six have three or four notes. In both, the largest ascending melodic movement is a major third. While there is one descending perfect fourth in each phrase in the FAR version, there is only one descending fourth in the fourth line of the Troyer. The melody of both versions spans an octave, the FAR from the B-flat just below middle C to the B-flat one octave higher. I have provided the first line of the FAR "Es sind" in order to compare this version with the Troyer version.

A further comparison, in table 3.1, points out the differences between the FAR song and the Troyer version, marking these with a double asterisk. These changes could be chalked up to Jackson's "vocal vagaries" or may represent group or self-expression.

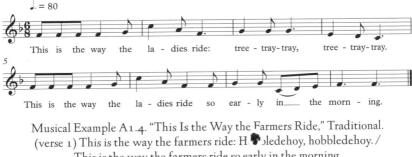

Musical Example A1.4. "This Is the Way the Farmers Ride," Traditional.
(verse 1) This is the way the farmers ride: H bledehoy, hobbledehoy. /
This is the way the farmers ride so early in the morning.
(verse 3) This is the way the gentlemen ride: Gallop-a-trot, gallop-a-trot. /
This is the way the gentlemen ride so early in the morning.
(verse 4) This is the way the cowboys ride: Hi, ho, Silver, AWAY!

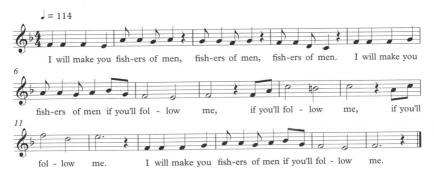

Musical Example A1.5. "Fishers of Men," Wayne County (2001).

The three versions of "Schlof, Bubeli, Schlof" differ widely in melodic material (see table 4.2). Comparing the intervals, there is a preponderance of major seconds in each but a greater variety of larger intervals in the Klassen version. As in "Mary Had a Little Lamb," Barbara's version, the essence of simplicity uses only three notes, all major seconds. Like most of Amish singing, all the notes are diatonic, which means that the melody conforms to the Western major scale and uses no accidental notes foreign to the key.

Musical Example A1.6. "In der stillen Einsamkeit"—"At the Cross,"
Holmes County (2001).

Musical Example A1.7. "Schaffet, schaffet, meine Kinder," Holmes County (2010).
Translation: *Create, create, my children,*
Create your blessedness (salvation):
Do not build, like impudent sinners,
Only for the present time,
But look to yourselves,
Struggle for heaven,
And strive also on earth.

Musicologist George Pullen Jackson documents four current Amish tunes as sixteenth-century folksongs, including "Hildebrand" for *Ausbund* hymn 119. Jackson identifies "Von Herzen woll'n wir singen" (*Ausbund* 692) (E♭-F-G-F-E♭-F-A♭-G♭-F-G♮-A♭-A♭-B♭-D♭-C-B♭-B♭-C-B♭-A♭-B♭-A♭-B♭-C-B♭-A♭-F-G♭-F-E♭-F-E♭) as a hymn based on "Hildebrand" (E♭-G♭-G♭-A♭-A♭-B♭-B♭ / B♭-B♭-C-D♭-B♭-B♭). He matches the first note sung on each syllable grouping (I have underlined them) in the Amish hymn to the melody line of "Hildebrand" from Erk and Böhme's collection of German folksongs in three volumes. Yes, some do match. But there isn't enough similarity to make a strong case. Erk and Böhme published lyrics they dated to the ninth century and paired them with the "Hildebrand" tune that they described as "widely sung in the 14th to 17th centuries."[1] Jackson makes a tenuous case for a historical connection and expresses amazement that the tune endured for 600 years.[2] But an equal case could be made that the typical rise and fall of any number of melodies shaped this *Ausbund* tune.

Musical Example A1.8. "O Gott Vater ins Himmels Throne," Holmes County (2011).
Translation: *O God Father in Heaven's Throne,*
Who has prepared a crown for us,
If we remain in Thy Son,
With Him here endure the cross and suffering,
In this life we yield to him,
And after his fellowship always strive.

A comparison between the Iowa and Indiana *Lobsang* examples (1938), the Holmes County (2006), and the Troyer (1997) shows three begin on *do*, but the Holmes County version has an additional perfect fourth (*sol*) as a lead-in to the *do*. Each version has one or two notes that the others do not. I have marked an "X" above these notes. For this evaluation, I have transposed all versions into the key of C even though they were not sung in the same key originally (Musical Example A1.9).

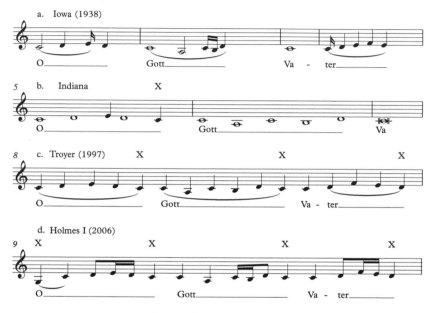

Musical Example A1.9. *Lobsang* openings.

Musical Example A1.10. "So will ichs aber heben an," verse 4, Holmes County (2008). Sung by Atlee Miller, personal interview, 23 Jan. 2008.

Musical Example A1.11. "Gelobt sei Gott im höchsten Thron," Holmes County (2007). Source: Atlee Miller, personal interview, 4 May 2007.

Musical Example A1.12. "My mother's not dead," Holmes County (2006).

♩. = 100

Thank you, Moth-er for pray-ing for me. If you had not pray'd, then
where would I be? They call'd you old-fash-ion'd but you loved the Lord. And your
pray'rs found the Mas - ter as your tears touch'd the floor.

Musical Example A1.13. "Thank You, Mother, for Praying for Me," chorus, Wayne County (2006). Source: Unidentified Amish woman, personal interview, Sept. 2006.

(verse 2) Somebody, somewhere was praying that night
When I came in and saw the light.
Well, it must have been Mama. I heard her before.
As her prayers touched the Master,
Her tears touched the floor. CHORUS
(verse 3) As she held to the altar and wouldn't give in,
'Til all of her children were born again.
Just an old fashioned mama but she loved the Lord
As her prayers touched the Master,
Her tears touched the floor. CHORUS

♩ = 80

Die Welt ist nicht mein Heim, Ich wan-de-re nur hin durch, Mei-ne Schät-ze sind be
wahrt Hin - ü-ber ir-gend wo; Die En-gel win-ken mir, Dort von der Him-mels
tür, Und ich fühl nicht da - heim In der Welt nim-mer mehr.

Musical Example A1.14. "Die Welt ist nicht mein Heim," Holmes County (2010).

Musical Example A1.15. "Wo ist Jesus, mein Verlangen," Wayne County (March 2008).

Musical Example A1.16. "Von Himmel hoch da komm," Holmes County (2010).
Source: *Eine Unparteiische Liedersammlung*, 158.

Musical Example A1.17. "Heut fänget," Holmes County (2010).
Source: *Eine Unparteiische Liedersammlung*, 160.

Musical Example A1.18. "Ach bleib bei uns," Holmes County (2008).
Translation: *O, abide with us, Lord Jesus Christ,*
Because evening has now come;
Thy Godly Word, that shining Light,
Allow not to be extinguished within us.

Musical Example A1.19. "Lebt friedsam," Holmes County (2008).
Source: *Ausbund,* 786–89.

Musical Example A1.20. "Weil nun die Zeit," Holmes County (2008).

Source: *Ausbund*, 789–91.

Translation: *Now is the time we must part*
So we want God at this time
To graciously accompany
That we consider on and on
His Holy Word we have heard
In order to prepare ourselves.

Notes

1. Erk and Böhme, *Deutscher Liederhort*. Qtd. in Jackson, "The Strange Music," 284.
2. Ibid., 285–86.

APPENDIX II

Research Methods

I began this study when I encountered a few Amish acquaintances, friends of my friends, who talked openly with me about their singing experiences. Soon, the shape of a book unfolded, and I decided on a plan of action: I would conduct interviews with the Amish and visit Amish schools throughout Wayne and Holmes Counties. My main focus would be to interview Amish people about their musical practices and attend as many Amish life events as I could.

Dr. George Kreps and I team-taught an Amish course so I could gain the opportunity to read and study. I traveled to libraries in Walnut Creek, Elizabethtown, and Wooster as well as to the Lancaster Historical Society. I interviewed Amish men and women and a few formerly Amish people in a variety of settings in northeastern Ohio. From 1999 to 2000, four undergraduate assistants—Andrea Lucas, Patrice Trudell, Esther Diehl, and Autumn Stewart-Zimmerman—and I conducted fifty-six five- to twenty-minute face-to-face interviews at Amish-frequented auctions in Mt. Hope, Kidron, and Farmerstown and on the street on market days in Charm, Berlin, Walnut Creek, and Sugarcreek, Ohio.

Interviews with Amish Adults

We also interviewed individuals and families in their homes through either second-order or snowball sampling. First, we would talk with Amish people, mainly child-care providers, house cleaners, or nursing aides referred to us by our non-Amish friends. One student's sister had been dating an Amish boy, and his family agreed to talk with us. Or we conversed with Amish people who were involved in workshops, advisory groups, or public forums arranged by the Ohio State University Extension. These Amish people, in turn, recommended their neighbors and friends for us to interview. For example, an Amish woman might say, "I don't sing well, but Sarah Yoder loves to sing. She lives down Geyers Chapel [in a house] with a big white barn."[1] When I would visit these women and identify myself as an acquaintance of one of their friends, they would graciously stop whatever project they were involved in and invite me inside to chat. In another situation, we attended a weekend workshop at the Inn at Honey Run in Millersburg, Ohio, eating meals and talking at length with Jacob Beachy, an Amish bishop, his wife, Erma, and two other Amish couples. This led to an invitation to visit the Beachy home and Erma inviting some of her women friends and relatives to meet me. Patrice Trudell attended the Former Amish Reunion (FAR), a semiannual gathering of ex-Amish, which serves as extended family support for individuals and families who have left the Amish community. She engaged in a day of lengthy person-to-person and group interviews and recording hymn singing.

Amish informants enjoyed bringing out songbooks (with lyrics only) they had collected from bus rides to Iowa or Kentucky. Then, they sang for us their favorites, such as "Mockingbird Hill" and a Swiss ballad about a young lover lying in the graveyard. One informant insisted that we record an "important" song and began to sing the old camp song "Found a Peanut." We laughed together over childhood memories.

A few Amish people we approached hesitated to answer questions, especially when we took notes. Others were open to discussing singing, occasionally inviting us to walk a little out of the way so they could sing less conspicuously. For the lengthier interviews, researchers asked a set of questions about child-rearing practices, the kinds of songs sung to young children, and the importance of singing in Amish life. Such questions often led to other areas of discussion, such as wedding or funeral practices, gender roles, youthful rowdiness, reports of abuse in Amish families, and health issues. Interviewees were also asked to sing on tape. Most refused. In their own homes, Amish parents spoke about their experiences raising children and offered us refreshments, even inviting us to return for further discussion. I interviewed one Amish woman and her teenaged daughter several times a month over a one-year period.

To research the chapters on worship music and youth sings, I attended some worship events and sings, and I conducted personal interviews with community members about their experiences. Each interview or attendance at an event raised more questions.

Visiting Amish Schools

To gather information on school singing, I visited twenty-three schools, one to three times each, for a total of over fifty visits. When possible, I talked with teachers, but mainly I observed morning openings and the first half of the school day. I talked with several teachers in their homes.

In school, as in other areas of their life, the Amish are very protective of their children. They understand that early experience has a powerful influence on a child's acceptance of the Amish tradition. Amish teachers are responsible to their school boards and to the parents for their scholars' welfare. Consequently, they shield their charges from outside influences. Yet, they did welcome me as a guest. I visited several schools by invitation of friends or family of Amish schoolteachers; in other cases, I stopped into a school in the morning just before the school day began and asked if I might listen to the children's singing. One young teacher spoke without embarrassment and with great enthusiasm: "You're interested in singing? You'll have to tell us how we compare. You should go to Oak Grove. They sing really well." She proceeded to give me directions to that school. Most Amish teachers even asked me to sign their guestbook and merely asked me not to make a tape recording. My notetaking appeared to bother some of the teachers, so instead I would listen carefully and then hurry to my car and write down every detail I could remember. I would take my own copy of *Unparteiische Liedersammlung* and ask to see other song-books the children used. I borrowed song sheets from several schools and copied and returned them. Every one of these materials included only texts and no musical notation.

I visited an Amish public school that enrolled nearly all Amish students, one Mennonite private school that was also attended by many Amish children, and twenty-one Amish private schools. I visited two schools three times each, eight schools twice, then began visiting other schools on a one-time, drop-in basis. I also was invited to attend a Christmas program at the Amish public school, with ap-proximately 150 Amish family members and 20 English guests, mostly family and friends of the conservative Mennonite teachers. Table A2.1 shows in brief the mu-sical practices of the twenty-three schools I visited. All the schools own and some-times use the *Unparteiische Liedersammlung*. A few, particularly the more conserva-tive, sing only from that book and only in German.

Finally, after reading about the Amish and talking with other researchers, I wrote articles and chapters and shared these with my Amish and non-Amish friends for review and suggestions for improvement. Often, these discussions would lead me to ask further questions. Sometimes, they would lead to an invitation to another

Table A2.1 School song titles with topics

English songs (topic)	German songs (topic)
At Calvary (salvation)	An Jesum denken oft und viel (devotion)
Boys and Girls for Jesus (salvation)	Bedenke Mensch, das Ende (death, salvation)
Christmas program:	
Twinkle, Christmas Star	Das Wort der Wahrheit
Silent Night	Es sind zween Weg (salvation)
Away in a Manger	
Joy to the World	
Hark the Herald Angels Sing	
Beautiful Star of Bethlehem	
So Have a Super, Duper Christmas with Jesus	
[All in various costumes throughout presentation, including camouflage for Silent Night]	

Table A2.1 (*cont.*)

English songs (topic)	German songs (topic)
Deep and Wide (salvation)	O Gott Vater, wir loben dich (praise)
From Jerusalem to Jericho (Bible story)	O Vater! Kindlich beten wir
Happy Birthday to You (fun, community)	Schaffet, schaffet, meine Kinder (salvation)
Have a Little Talk with Jesus (devotion)	Wir singen dir, Immanuel and Hallelujah (praise)
I Feel Like Travelin' On (heaven)	Wo ist Jesus mein Verlangen (devotion)
I Know Who Hung the Stars (praise)	Zu sing'n hab ich im Sinn
I Need No Mansion Here Below (heaven, faithfulness)	Gott ist die Liebe (God's love)
I Was Made in His Likeness (service)	In der stillen Einsamkeit (devotion) with "Father I Adore Thee" in one version
In Life's Morning (service)	
Jesus Loves Me [with American Sign Language] (devotion)	
My Life Is a Canvas (service)	
Now the Sun Is Shining (thanks)	
Peter, James, and John [with action] (Bible story)	
Shadows Are Falling (heaven)	
Singing, Singing, Voices Ringing (praise)	
The Old Ballgame (Fun, Community)	
The Other Day, I Saw a Bear (fun)	
The Wonder of Love (devotion)	
There's a Bluebird on Your Windowsill (gratitude)	
Thirty Pieces of Silver (salvation, faithfulness)	
This Land Is Your Land (stewardship)	
Where Would I Go but to the Lord? (devotion)	
Who Made the Flowers? (praise)	

Amish event. I attended every activity to which I was invited (except for one eightieth birthday party because I was out of the country) and then consulted with Amish friends to discuss what I had observed. From the beginning of my research to the present, I have tried to listen carefully, and as a result, my respect for these Amish friends and acquaintances has grown. I am grateful for the hours they gave me and for the opportunities I have had to share their lives.

Note

1. Unidentified Amish woman, personal interview, August 1999.

Historical Studies of Amish Music

Rudolf Wolkan organized and published the first scholarly work that documents the origins of Anabaptist hymns and describes the lives of hymn writers. Writing from the University of Vienna, Wolkan separated the hymns of the Anabaptists from those of the Swiss Brethren and Hutterites in *Die Lieder der Wiedertäufer, Ein Beitrag zur deutschen und niederländischen Literatur- und Kirchengeschichte*.[1]

With few exceptions, the most recent scholarly writings on Amish music date to nearly fifty years ago. Prior to the 1960s, the Amish community drew the interest of several noted musicologists, such as Bruno Nettl and George Pullen Jackson, and literary scholars like John Umble. These scholars generally studied the hymns of the *Ausbund* in their historical, but not social, context. From Wolkan to the present, this appendix surveys the literature that undergirds the current study.

Ernst Correll's 1930 "The Value of Hymns for Mennonite History" shows how the "Zürich Lied" of the sixteenth century details martyrdoms by starvation, beheading, and other methods of persecution in the Zürich penitentiary. Through reading these hymns, Correll proposes, historians may understand the "Anabaptist troubles" of the sixteenth and early seventeenth century. These texts prove that authorities continued their "intense efforts to quiet down the Anabaptist protest," which led to interference by the government to rescue their Mennonite subjects. Another consequence was the Anabaptist exodus to several German states and on to Pennsylvania.[2] Correll verifies that Swiss authorities seized and destroyed all hymnals and song booklets they found in order to limit the spread of their dangerous message. Correll's work does not analyze any musical aspects of these hymns.

In 1939, John Umble published "The Old Order Amish, Their Hymns and Hymn Tunes" in the *Journal of American Folk-Lore* (now the *Journal of American Folklore*). This article includes a history of the *Ausbund*. In discussing the tunes of the *Ausbund* hymns, Umble lists several of the tune titles given in the *Ausbund*. He mentions that Alan Lomax recorded ten or twelve tunes near Goshen in 1938 for the Library of Congress and notes the resemblance between those melodies and Gregorian chant.[3] He adds a transcription of a Christian hymn and two transcriptions from Lomax's recordings of *Vorsingers* singing the *Loblied*, "O God, Father, we praise Thee."[4] There are subtle differences of embellishments between the renditions, which Umble attributes to "freedom in the interpretation of the melody."[5]

Musicologist George Pullen Jackson wrote his doctoral dissertation on Amish hymnology in 1945. He transcribed the tunes for nearly a hundred *Ausbund* hymns. He documents seventy-five tunes that *Ausbund* authors or hymn collectors paired with hymn texts. Jackson mentions that Joseph W. Yoder created his book *Amische Lieder* by asking his friends to sing each hymn numerous times while he transcribed them. In this way, Yoder bypassed making voice recordings, of which the Amish disapprove. In his analysis, Jackson describes Amish group singing as "uncontrolled (by instrument, director, or notation)" and says "it drags." This slow singing causes pitch variations as one singer waits for the others to change to the next pitch in the melody. The variations become waverings or "vocal vagaries" that become "fixed, stylized, incorporated with their 'tunes,' and a singing *manner* is born—or evolves," Jackson postulates.[6] As touched on in chapter 8, the origin and evolution of the hymn tunes also captured his imagination as he tried to unearth German folksongs from which the Amish hymn tunes borrow.

In 1949, linguist J. William Frey published his chapter "Amish Hymns as Folk Music" in *Pennsylvania Songs and Legends*. Frey describes worship singing practices, including eight transcriptions from the Library of Congress's Alan Lomax collection of Amish hymns. Frey often titles them according to their set position in a worship gathering—for example, "First Hymn at Communion" for "O Gott Vater ins Himmels Throne."[7] He also discusses the origin and content of the *Ausbund* hymn texts. Of the tunes the Amish use when singing the hymns, Frey explains, "A few were sung to original melodies, but nearly all of them were set to the popular religious and secular tunes of the day. Among those of a religious nature was the well-known Lutheran hymn 'Ein feste Burg ist unser Gott,' which furnishes the melody for a number of the Amish hymns. The majority, as the *Ausbund* itself often suggests at the head of a hymn . . . was based on secular and popular folksongs. The most popular air, judging from the number of hymns that were set to it, seems to have been 'By the Waters of Babylon.'"[8]

Frey mentions specific songs used at evening sings, such as "Wo ist Jesus, mein Verlangen," which he translates as "Where is Jesus, My Desire." Hymn tunes such as "Sweet Hour of Prayer" are used for "Du unbegreiflich höchstes Gut" ("Thou Inconceivably Wonderful Blessing") and "From Greenland's Icy Mountains" for "Ermuntert euch, ihr Frommen!" ("Awake, Ye Pious Christians!"). He also comments that Amish youth employ harmonicas and "hillbilly" tunes, such as the then-popular ballad, "The Death of Floyd Collins" (Musical Example A3.1).

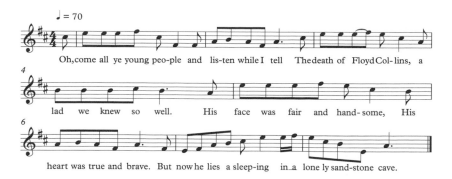

Musical Example A3.1. "The Death of Floyd Collins." Source: Wolf, "The Death of Floyd Collins," www.lyon.edu/wolfcollection/songs/gingerdeath1266.html.

Frey notes that Amish youth add a verse to the ballad that lends a plain religious and moral message to this song:

> Young people, oh, take warning,
> Of Floyd Collins' fate;
> And give your heart to Jesus,
> Before it is too late.
> It may not be a sand cave,
> In which we find our tomb;
> But at the bar of judgments,
> We too must meet our doom.[9]

Frey also documents the publication of *Ein Unparteyisches Gesang-Buch*, a non-denominational or "impartial" songbook, by Old Order Mennonites in Lancaster, Pennsylvania, in 1804.[10] This song collection greatly influences the content of other collections, such as the *Liedersammlung*.

Charles Burkhart's master's thesis, "The Music of the Old Amish and the Old Colony Mennonites: A Contemporary Monodic Practice," written in 1952, describes several Amish activities in which singing figures prominently. Reconstructing from *Rosanna's Boys*, a novel by Amish writer Joseph W. Yoder, Burkhart outlines the typical Sunday worship gathering, a youth singing on the evening of worship, and a wedding service, listing the hymns sung for each. He describes communion services continuing late into the afternoon, complete with the ritual of footwashing, women with women and men with men, inspired by Jesus's taking up basin and towel and washing the feet of his own disciples.[11] Burkhart presents hymns for the occasions of communion, the reinstatement of a backslider, and funeral services.

Burkhart enumerates the hymnbooks used by the Amish, particularly the *Ausbund* and the *Unparteiische Liedersammlung*, first published in Lancaster in 1860 with both texts of "slow" songs from the *Ausbund* and "fast" songs from Mennonite hymnals. In 1892, the Iowa Amish enlarged the book to include more of both song types as well as British and American hymns. This version is called the Gingerich (or Guengerich) edition. Later editions of this hymnbook add more songs suited to special occasions, such as weddings and communion.

Burkhart notes that, although the *Ausbund* gives no musical notation, a tune name appears under each title. These tunes date to the sixteenth century, and there has been some effort but little success in tracing the original tunes. He relates that other tunes for these hymns were probably folk tunes adapted to the structures and needs of the hymn text. Burkhart discusses theories as to the origin and development of the current melodies, from Gregorian chant to folk melodies with "tone-additions" over time. Burkhart also explores how singing is taught to the young, as well as typical singing styles and techniques, as mentioned in chapter 3. He incorporates transcriptions of hymns recorded by John Umble and Leland Byler at an Amish gathering in Iowa in 1939.

Harold S. Bender wrote about "The Hymnology of the Anabaptists" in 1957, documenting various Anabaptist hymnbooks, including "a written one and a printed one" from 1598 Württemberg. He tells of one early hymn writer, prisoner-martyr George Blaurock, who died in 1529. The martyr songs "sang themselves into the hearts of many, clothed in popular tunes," Bender notes.[12] Those who heard, he claims, sang and were moved to belief and willingness to die for their faith. Bender describes it as "unfortunate" that the Mennonites of Holland, Germany, and Russia did not continue to sing these hymns because they turned to using state church hymnals.

In his 1957 article "The Hymns of the Amish: An Example of Marginal Survival," musicologist Bruno Nettl seeks to establish that isolated groups may be able to preserve a "lost" historical musical style.[13] Just as Francis J. Child came to the hollows of rural Appalachia to collect Scottish ballads and found that immigrants had preserved texts, tunes, and styles for more than a century, Nettl states that Amish singing styles have stayed virtually the same for centuries.

Nettl notes that High German has become for the Amish an "esoteric language comparable to Latin in the Roman Catholic Church."[14] Few understand it or can read it, but the Amish sing their worship songs in High German. Nettl discusses the tempo, rhythm, melodic contour, cadences, forms, *Vorsingers*, major scales, melismas, ornamentations, and the monophonic nature of the hymns. He summarizes theories as to the origins of the tunes and includes a transcription of an Amish hymn from a recording in the National Archives of American Folksong. He describes the tunes as connected to European folk hymns, church music, and Baroque styles of ornamentation.

Rupert Hohmann's dissertation, "The Church Music of the Old Order Amish of the United States" (1959), also focuses on the history and tunes of *Ausbund* hymns. Citing Johannes Zahn's *Die Melodien der deutschen evangelischen Kirchenlieder*, a six-volume collection of German chorales, folksongs, and music of the Roman Catholic Church, along with Franz Boehme's *Altdeutches Liederbuch* and Ludwig Erk and Boehme's *Deutscher Liederhort*, Hohmann identifies root melodies for fifty-four

Ausbund hymns.[15] He analyzes and compares ornamentation, melodic arcs, ranges, modalities, interval use, *musica ficta*, repetition, sequencing, phrase beginnings, and cadences in hymns from Pennsylvania, Iowa, and Kansas communities. He shows that the ornamentation in Iowa and Kansas has more complexity, while the Pennsylvanian Amish employ stepwise ornamentation and sing more slowly. Hohmann finds the rhythm of Amish singing to be "capricious and subtle" and observes that the Amish use few dynamic nuances.[16]

In "The Amish" (1950), the third chapter in his book *The Pennsylvania Dutch*, Fredric Klees offers a brief discussion of the music of worship services. Noting that the Amish do not use musical notation in their *Ausbund* hymnbooks, Klees relates, "The tunes have been handed down from one generation to another and in certain instances have undergone so great a change as to make them unrecognizable . . . The style of singing is slow and doleful. A leader plunges into the melody, the others joining in. There is no part singing, for this is ruled out as a worldly innovation. There are no choirs in an Amish meeting and no organs or musical instruments of any kind. Though many of the Amish show astonishing skill in singing, a man who is able to lead the singing in meeting is regarded with real respect."[17] Klees remarks how several of the songs used for Sunday evening singing are musical variations of ballads and hymns. Klees makes a glancing reference to hymns sung in wedding services and mentions the names of several youth singing games such as "Skip to My Lou."

As noted in chapter 3, Hedwig Durnbaugh's "The Amish Singing Style: Theories of Its Origin and Description of Its Singularity" (1999) is one of the few recent examinations of Amish singing. Durnbaugh argues that the hymn tunes have changed from the ones noted in margins of early *Ausbunds* to such a degree as to make them unrecognizable. But, it is safe to say that at least in the past ninety years, there has been a great deal of continuity of tunes. Because she is a Baroque specialist, Durnbaugh's work focuses on ornamentations of the tunes. She concludes that the original Amish sang in a syllabic style but that extra notes (diminutions) crept in and became codified into the Amish tune styles of today.

Each of these researchers worked to describe the music sung in Amish worship services, but they gave scant attention to songs sung outside the worship setting. As a result of this review, it becomes clear that there are many aspects of Amish singing meriting further study. A study of the literature has helped to shape the research direction of this book, describing and analyzing singing through the Amish life cycle.

Notes

1. Wolkan, *Die Lieder der Wiedertäufer*.
2. Correll, "The Value of Hymns," 215–19.
3. Umble, "The Old Order Amish," 92.
4. *Ausbund*, 770.
5. Umble, "The Old Order Amish," 95.
6. Jackson, "The Strange Music," 278–79.
7. Frey, "Hymns as Folk Music," 156.

8. Ibid., 149.

9. Ibid, 151–53.

10. Ibid., 142.

11. John 13:2–20.

12. Bender, "Hymnology of the Anabaptists," 5–10.

13. Nettl, "Hymns of the Amish," 323.

14. Ibid., 324.

15. Zahn, *Melodien der deutschen evangelischen*. Boehme, *Altdeutsches Liederbuch*. Erk and Boehme, *Deutscher Liederhort*. These volumes catalog hymns from the thirteenth to the eighteenth centuries.

16. Hohmann, "Music of the Old Order," 58.

17. Klees, "The Amish," in *The Pennsylvania Dutch*.

Notes

Where two editions of a book are given, page numbers cited are from the more recent edition.

Chapter 1. Who Are the Amish?

Epigraph. Eine Unparteiische Liedersammlung, 156 (1999 edition). First printed in 1860 by John Baer's Sons of Lancaster, this is a condensed version of *Unpartheyisches Gesang-Buch,* containing 47 songs from the *Ausbund* and 104 from later sources. It is known among the Amish as "das kleine Büchlein" or "dinn Blichi" because of its size. Ohio Amish Library, *Songs of the Ausbund,* 4n; translation by Martina Machniak.

1. *Eine Unparteiische Liedersammlung,* 156.

2. The date of Jacob Amman's death is unknown.

3. For more detail on the European origins of the Amish and their immigration to North America, see Kraybill, Johnson-Weiner, and Nolt, *The Amish,* chapters 2 and 3.

4. For current Amish demographics and population statistics, visit www.etown.edu /Amishstudies/.

5. See Hurst and McConnell, *An Amish Paradox,* for a detailed description of the Amish affiliations living in Holmes County, Ohio. Kraybill, Johnson-Weiner, and Nolt, in *The Amish,* provide a description of North American Amish tribes.

6. Unidentified Amish woman, personal interview, 19 March 2008. I identify by name all Amish interviewees who specifically agreed to be mentioned; otherwise, I have maintained their privacy.

7. Rokicky, *Creating a Perfect World,* 5.

8. Hurst and McConnell, *An Amish Paradox* provide an excellent description and analysis of recent changes in the Holmes County settlement.

9. Marglin, "Development as Poison," 25.

10. Unidentified Amish woman, personal Interview, 22 July 1999.

11. Pamuk, *Istanbul,* 244.

12. Foucault, *Madness and Civilization,* 20.

13. Smucker, "How Amish Children View," 220.

14. Hostetler and Huntington, *Amish Children,* 21–22.

15. E., J. H. "Abner and His Cookies," 27–28.

16. Piaget, *The Origins of Intelligence*, 335.

17. Smucker, "How Amish Children View," 220.

18. Milicia, *Amish Teens Rebel.*

19. Erikson, *Childhood and Society*, 266–68.

20. Unidentified Amish men and women. Personal interviews between 2000 and 2007.

21. Hurst and McConnell in *An Amish Paradox* and Kraybill, Johnson-Weiner, and Nolt in *The Amish* provide information on Amish schools in Holmes County and across the nation, respectively.

22. Fishman, *Language in Sociocultural Change*, 25. See also Keim, "From Erlanbach to New Glarus," 9.

23. Gallagher, "Accepting Things Modern."

24. *Family Life, Young Companion,* and/or *Blackboard Bulletin* can be ordered from Pathway Publishers, 10380 Carter Road, Aylmer, Ontario N5H 2R3 Canada for $11.00, $8.00, and $7.00 per year, respectively, or $21.00 per year for all three. In Canada add 6% G.S.T.

25. Amish man, personal interview, 29 October 1999.

26. Amish woman, personal interview, 22 July 1999.

27. Interviews of Amish adults at Mt. Hope, Middletown, and Berlin, summer 1999.

28. *Christenpflicht.*

29. Geertz, "Religion as a Cultural System," 14. Geertz, *The Interpretation of Cultures*, 90.

30. McNamara, "Introduction," 5–6.

31. Weber, qtd. in Geertz, *The Interpretation of Cultures*, 131.

32. Nolt, *History of the Amish.*

33. Kauffman, *Amish in Eastern Ohio*, 8.

34. Geertz, *The Interpretation of Cultures*, 14.

35. Hostetler, *Educational Achievement and Lifestyles*, 406–7.

36. Hostetler, *Educational Achievement and Lifestyles*, 6.

37. Mast, *The Duty of Children*, qtd. in Hostetler, *Educational Achievement and Lifestyles*, 400.

Chapter 2. The Functions of Amish Singing

Epigraph. Ausbund, Lied 50, 275 (1997 edition).

1. Unidentified Amish woman, personal interview, 29 October 1999.

2. Results from a survey conducted at Mt. Hope Auction in August 1999.

3. Blacking, *Music, Culture, and Experience*, 34.

4. Unidentified Amish people, personal interviews, summer 1999.

5. Wittmer and Moser, "Counseling the Old Order," 266.

6. Rose, *Governing the Soul*, 50.

7. Thomas A. Dorsey (1899–1993), an American songwriter known as the father of gospel music, was a preacher's son who became a pianist for blues artists Bessie Smith and Gertrude "Ma" Rainey.

8. Raber, *Music—Harmonizing*, 5–6.

9. Brunk, *Musical Instruments*, 3.

10. Ada Lendon, personal interview, 26 July 1999.

11. Blacking, *Music, Culture, and Experience*, 217.

12. "The Stranger and His Music," 14–16.

13. Unidentified Amish woman, personal interview, 29 October 1999.

14. Unidentified Amish woman, personal interview, 21 April 2007.

15. Teacher Arlene, "The Singing Situation," 4.

16. Stokes, *Ethnicity, Identity and Music*, 6–8.

17. Kingston, "The Amish Story," n.p.

18. Hostetler and Huntington, *Amish Children*, 14.

19. Blacking, *Venda Children's Song*, 31.

20. Kraybill, *Concise Encyclopedia of Amish*, 20.

21. Huntington, "The Amish Family," 1.

22. Behaque, *Music and Black Ethnicity*, 20, 32.

23. See Keeney, *Dutch Anabaptist Thought*, 14 and Oyer, "Amish Theology?" 281.

24. Yoder, *Amische Lieder*, preface.

25. Blacking, *Music, Culture, and Experience*, 56.

26. Behaque, *Music and Black Ethnicity*, v, 13. See also Blacking, "The Study of Man," 3–17.

27. Blacking, "The Study of Man," 3–15.

28. Keil, *Tiv Song*, 254–57.

29. Blacking, *Music, Culture, and Experience*, 198.

30. Blacking, "A Commonsense View," 98.

31. Blacking, *Music, Culture, and Experience*, 26, 127.

32. Fishman, *Amish Literacy*. Fishman notes that the average hymn has 17.6 stanzas. John Hostetler explains that the Amish "rarely sing more than four or five verses of a hymn," but some hymns "have as many as thirty-seven verses." See Hostetler, *Amish Society*, 230.

33. Nettl, *The Study of Ethnomusicology*, 92–95.

34. Grauer, "Thoughts on Cross Cultural," 3.

35. Blacking, "Ethnography of Musical Performance," 384.

36. Blacking, *Music, Culture, and Experience*, 172.

37. Blacking, *Music, Culture, and Experience*, 160–62.

Chapter 3. Case Study: "Es sind zween Weg"

Epigraph. "Es sind zween Weg," *Eine Unparteiische Liedersammlung*, 151.

1. *Ausbund*, 748; *Liedersammlung*, 156.

2. These include: "See, I have set before you this day life and good and death and evil; In that I command you this day to love the Lord your God, to walk in God's ways, and to keep God's commandments and God's judgments, that you may live and multiply . . . I have set before you life and death, blessing and cursing; therefore choose life, that both you and your children may live." Deuteronomy 30:15, 16, 19; "And turn ye not aside: for then you will go after vain things, which cannot profit or deliver; for they are vain . . . Moreover as for me, God forbid that I should sin against the Lord in ceasing to pray for you: but I will teach you the good and the right way; only fear the Lord, and serve him in truth with all your heart: for consider how great things he hath done for you." 1 Samuel 12:21–24 (ca. 1095 B.C.E.); "Hast thou marked the old ways, which wicked men have trodden?" Job 22:15 (ca. 1520 B.C.E.); "Remove from me the way of lying . . . I have chosen the way of truth." Psalm 119:29 (ca. 1030 B.C.E.); "Stand ye in the ways, and see, and ask for the old paths, where is the good way, and walk therein, and ye shall find rest for your souls." Jeremiah 6:16 (ca. 601 B.C.E.).

3. Harms, *Homo Viator in Bivio*, 40–43.

4. Sommers, "Teaching the Virtues," 41.

5. Harms, *Homo Viator in Biviio*, 85.

6. Meyers, "The Amish Division," 40–53.

7. Miller, *A Pilgrim's Search*, n.p.

8. See appendix I, Musical Example A1.3 for an additional version of the song—from a songbook compiled by Ben Troyer in 1997—and a comparison between it and the FAR version.

9. Blacking, *Venda Children's Songs*, 156.

10. Yoder, *Amische Lieder*, 25.

11. Yoder, *Amische Lieder*, v.

12. Steel, "Shape Note Singing Schools."

13. Troyer, Ausbund *and* Liedersammlung *Songs*, iii.

14. Troyer, Ausbund *and* Liedersammlung *Songs*, iii.

15. Jackson, "Amish Medieval Folk Tunes," 152.

16. Umble, "The Old Order Amish," 92.

17. Frey, "Hymns as Folk Music," 155.

18. Burkhart, "The Church Music," 34.

19. Nettl, "Hymns of the Amish," 323.

20. Durnbaugh, "The Amish Singing Style," 29.

21. Nettl, "Hymns of the Amish," 325.

22. Jackson, Amish Medieval Folk Tunes, 286–88.

Chapter 4. Songs for Nurture

Epigraph. Words, spelling, and translation provided by an Amish friend, Ada Lendon.

1. Jacob and Erma Beachy, personal interview, September 1999.

2. Yoder and Estes, eds., *Proceedings of the Amish*, 180.

3. Hostetler and Huntington, *Amish Children*, 14–16.

4. O'Day, *Family and Family Relationships*, 39.

5. Huntington, "The Amish Family," 384.

6. Atlee Miller, personal interview, 2 May 2007.

7. "The Problem Corner," *Family Life*, 31–32.

8. Hostetler, *Amish Society*, 156.

9. Huntington, "The Amish Family," 386.

10. Hostetler, *Amish Society*, 157.

11. Unidentified Amish woman, personal interview, 22 July 1999.

12. Titon, *Worlds of Music*, 495.

13. Blacking, "Problem of Music Description," 54–72.

14. Sackville-West, *Nursery Rhymes*, 27.

15. Sackville-West, *Nursery Rhymes*, 29.

16. Sackville-West, *Nursery Rhymes*, 30.

17. Sackville-West, *Nursery Rhymes*, 20.

18. Gerstner-Hirzel, *Das volkstümliche deutsche Wiegenlied*, 243, 271–72, 275, 323.

19. Klassen, *Singing Mennonite*, 29–31.

20. Klassen, *Singing Mennonite*, 29–31.

21. The speed is quarter note = 176.

22. Unidentified Amish informants, personal interviews, July, August 1999.

23. Ibid.

Chapter 5. Songs for Instruction

Unparthenisches Gesang-Buch, 151.

1. Apel, *Harvard Dictionary of Music*, 626–27.
2. "Summary," 30.
3. Giroux, *Border Crossings*, 76–77.
4. Hostetler and Huntington, *Children in Amish Society*, 109.
5. Kraybill and Bowman, *Backroad to Heaven*, 103–5.
6. Hostetler, *Amish Society*, 156.
7. Klimuska, *Amish One-Room Schools*, n.p.
8. Klimuska, *Amish One-Room Schools*, n.p.
9. These songs are generally sung slower than quarter note = 80 beats per minute.

Chapter 6. Case Study: School Repertoire

Eine Unparteiische Liedersammlung, 176 (1999 edition). Translation by Martina Machniak. Tune: "Jesus, Lover of My Soul," according to Frey, "Hymns as Folk Music," 151.

1. Ressler, "*Liedersammlung's* 175th Anniversary," 18.
2. I have noted this example as the children sang it. Since they held no phrase ending more than one beat, it gave the feeling of alternating four and three beat phrases. The sound is very smooth, not choppy, however.
3. Fisher and Stahl, *The Amish School*, 25.
4. Coblentz, *Music in a Biblical Perspective*, 9.
5. Coblentz, *Music in a Biblical Perspective*, 44.
6. Teacher Arlene, "The Singing Situation," 4.

Chapter 7. Songs of Identity

David Beatty wrote this song in 1958. The Oak Ridge Boys and several gospel groups have since recorded it.

1. Unidentified Amish man, personal interview, 9 April 2008.
2. Unidentified Amish woman, personal interview, 18 March 2008.
3. *Inspiring Favorites* is published by a committee of the Markham-Waterloo Mennonite Conference of Ontario.

Chapter 8. Songs of Memory

Ausbund, Hymn 87, 453, translated in Miller, *Our Heritage, Hope and Faith*, 190.

1. Atlee and Mary Miller, personal interviews, 4 May 2007.
2. See Rokicky, *Creating a Perfect World*; Alpert, "Heart and Soul," www.bbc.co.uk/programmes/p005qznm; Bruce, *And They Sang Hallelujah*.
3. Unidentified Amishman, personal interview, August 1999.
4. Umble, "The Old Order Amish," 85.
5. Yoder, "The *Ausbund*."
6. *Ausbund*, 435. Smith, *The Mennonite Immigration*, 255.
7. Ohio Amish Library, *Songs of the Ausbund*, 4.
8. Umble, "The Old Order Amish," 87.
9. Umble, "The Old Order Amish," 6.

10. Frey, "Hymns as Folk Music," 142.

11. Springer, "Editions of the *Ausbund*," 32–39.

12. Bender, "Teachings Stressed in the *Ausbund*," 20–22.

13. Frey, "Hymns as Folk Music," 142.

14. Riall and Peters, *Hymns of the* Ausbund, 33.

15. Riall and Peters, *Hymns of the* Ausbund, 135.

16. Yoder, "The *Ausbund*," 8–10.

17. Yoder, "The *Ausbund*," 9.

18. Yoder, "The *Ausbund*," 10.

19. Wolkan, *Die Lieder der Wiedertäufer*, 151–52.

20. Martin Luther himself set some of his texts to folk tunes of his day. Musical borrowing has been a standard practice since early days. See Blume, *Protestant Church Music* and Harrell, *Martin Luther, His Music*.

21. Wolkan, *Die Lieder der Wiedertäufer*, 151–52.

22. Songs with each of the ranges include the following: range of a fifth, 1 song; sixth, 12; seventh, 6; octave, 27; ninth, 19; tenth, 3; and twelfth, 2. One song with the range of a twelfth, "Ew'ger Vater," also has an interesting set of intervals. The piece opens outlining a major triad, C-E-G, surrounds the C and descends by seconds to the C, then moves to C-E-G and falls from G to C. The third line has a downward melody of C-A-F. Most of the piece moves by step, but the movement by thirds outlining triads is unusual. The Anabaptists named this tune "Grasshopper Weisz." Of forty syllables per verse, nine have three notes, seven have four, four have five, four have seven, and two have eight notes. For this song, the Amish sing twenty-six of the syllables to three or more notes. By contrast, "All die ihr jetz" is syllabic, which means it has one or two notes per syllable. In its twenty-six syllables, which have a range of only a sixth, one has five notes, two have four, four have three, twelve have two, and seven have one.

23. Frey, "Hymns as Folk Music," 142.

24. Atlee Miller, personal interview, March 2007.

25. Umble, "The Old Order Amish," 87.

26. Ohio Amish Library, *Songs of the* Ausbund, 3.

Chapter 9. Songs of Belonging

Eine Unparteiische Liedersammlung, 80 (1999 edition).

1. Unidentified Amish woman, personal interview, October 2006.

2. Ibid.

3. Other songs used during the service are *Ausbund* 359, 408, 604, 655, and 770.

4. Episcopal Church, *The Hymnal*, 409.

5. 1 Peter 5:14.

6. *Christenpflicht*, 42.

7. *Ausbund* hymn 99, p. 526, vs. 20, 21, trans. Miller, *Our Heritage, Hope and Faith*, 293.

8. Atlee Miller, personal interview, 4 May 2007.

9. Before his execution, Jesus shares bread and wine with his disciples and asks them to solidify their commitment to spreading the message of a new kingdom, a new world order. The fourth gospel, attributed to John, reports that Jesus also washes their feet as a sign of humility (John 13:4–20).

Chapter 10. Case Study: The *Loblied*, or *Lobsang*

Ausbund, 770 (1997 edition).

1. Wolkan, *Die Lieder der Wiedertäufer*, 118–19. Ohio Amish Library, *Songs of the Ausbund*, 3–4.

2. Jackson, "Amish Medieval Folk Tunes," 152.

3. The grace notes appear as small notes. Like a cut in Irish bagpipe music, a grace note with a slash through the stem precedes the beat and anticipates the main note, which follows on the beat. Glissandos, or slides between two notes, occur between almost all intervals that are farther apart than one musical step. The first glissando occurs between the first two notes of the song (Musical Example 10.1). They are four steps apart.

4. However, the F-sharp also functions less as a raised note because the succeeding note is a lower pitch. The F-sharp does not lead to G, for example, but returns to an E.

5. In the Lomax, Indiana, version (1938b; Musical Example 10.3), the rhythm is static because the singers sustain very long notes, singing notes that neighbor each other, as in measure 4, where they walk up the scale from the whole note B to the whole note D. In measure 9, they leap down a third (from D to B) and turn around and sing a second higher (a C) as the third through fifth notes and the same turn for the next three notes. Yet, comparing the first measures of the Lomax (1938b) and Holmes County (2006) versions shows that the rhythm of long-short-long-short (L=long, S=short, Musical Example 10.3, first line, second through fifth notes) becomes LSSL in the Holmes County version (Musical Example 10.1, first line, third through sixth notes). As the song progresses, the Holmes County singer sometimes adjusts the notes so that the rhythm approaches that of the Lomax, long-short-long-long, in diminished note lengths.

6. Yoder, *Amische Lieder*, preface.

7. Smith, *Mennonite Immigration to Pennsylvania*, 256.

Chapter 11. Songs of Love and Life

Ohio Amish Library, *Songs of the* Ausbund, 141–43, verse 8.

1. The poetic Song of Solomon and Revelation 19:7–10 and 21:9ff are examples of passages commonly believed to refer to the Bride of Christ. Ohio Amish Library, *ibid.*, 141.

2. Stoll, *In Meiner Jugend*, 209.

3. *Unparteiische Liedersammlung*, Hymn 248, 385.

4. Klees, *The Pennsylvania Dutch*, 56.

5. Huntington, *Dove at the Window*, 164.

6. Translation from Belle Center Amish Church, Rushsylvania, Ohio, version (2003). Sugarcreek, OH: Carlisle, 452.

7. *Ausbund*, 227.

8. *Liedersammlung*, 189.

9. Unidentified Amish woman, personal interview, 4 May 2007.

10. Lyrics by Mrs. A. S. Bridgewater, written in the early twentieth century.

Chapter 12. Songs of Trust

Ausbund, 301 (1997 edition).

1. Lapp, *Heartland Hymns*, 451.

2. Unidentified Amish man, personal interview, August 1999.

3. The tune used for this hymn is "The Love of God," written by Frederick M. Lehman in 1917.

4. *Eine Unparteiische Liedersammlung*, 158.

5. Unidentified Amish woman, personal interview, 27 March 2007.

6. Unidentified Amish woman, personal interview by Patrice Trudell, 15 July 1999.

7. Erma Beachy, personal interview, 16 February 2007.

8. Ibid.

9. William B. Bradbury, born in Maine in 1816 and dying in New Jersey in 1868, wrote and compiled Sunday school hymns to promote devotional singing.

Chapter 13. Songs for the Future

Ausbund, 604 (1997 edition).

1. Blacking, "*A Commonsense View*," 23.

2. Levine, *Black Culture*, 5.

3. See Bender, "Teachings Stressed in the *Ausbund*," 20.

4. Numerous personal Amish interviews in 1999 and 2000.

5. Kraybill, Nolt, and Weaver-Zercher, *Amish Grace*, 20—21.

6. Translation by Martina Machniak.

7. Kraybill, Nolt, and Weaver-Zercher, *Amish Grace*, 28.

8. *Ausbund*, 242, hymn 44, verse 2.

Bibliography

Allgemeine Liedersammlung zum privaten und öffentlicher Gottes-Dienst, Die. Mennonitische Verlag-Handlung, 1877.

Alpert, Jessica. "Heart and Soul: The Whoop," BBC World Services. January 17, 2010. www.bbc.co.uk/programmes/p00b6dtf.

Amish Music Variety: Hymns to Harmonicas. Audio CD. Leola, PA: Harmonies Workshop, 1997.

Apel, Willi. *Harvard Dictionary of Music.* 2nd ed., Cambridge, MA: Belknap, 1969.

Ausbund, Das ist: Etliche schöne christliche Lieder. Lancaster, PA: Amish Book Committee, 1997. Originally published in 1564.

Behaque, G. H. *Music and Black Ethnicity: The Caribbean and South America.* New Brunswick: Transaction, 1994.

Bender, Elizabeth. "Teachings Stressed in the Ausbund." In *Four Hundred Years with the Ausbund,* by Paul M. Yoder, E. Bender, H. Graber, and N. P. Springer, 19–24. Scottdale, PA: Herald Press, 1964.

Bender, Harold S. "The Hymnology of the Anabaptists." *Mennonite Quarterly Review* 31 (Jan 1957): 5–10.

Blacking, John. "*A Commonsense View of All Music*": *Reflections on Percy Grainger's Contribution to Writings on Ethnomusicology and Music Education.* Cambridge: Cambridge University Press, 1987.

———. "Ethnography of Musical Performance." In *Report on the 12th International Musicological Society Congress (Berkeley, 1977),* edited by Daniel Heartz and Bonnie Wade, 383–401. Basel: Barenreiter Kassel, 1977.

———. *Music, Culture, and Experience: Selected Papers of John Blacking,* Reginald Byron, ed. Chicago: University of Chicago Press, 1995.

———. "The Problem of Music Description." In *Music, Culture, and Experience: Selected Papers of John Blacking,* edited by Reginald Byron, 54–72. Chicago: University of Chicago Press, 1995.

———. "The Study of Man as a Music Maker." In *The Performing Arts: Music and Dance,* edited by John Blacking and Joann W. Kealiinohomoku, 3–15. The Hague: Mouton, 1979.

———. *Venda Children's Song: A Study in Ethnomusicological Analysis.* Chicago: University of Chicago Press, 1967.

Blume, Friedrich. *Protestant Church Music*. New York: W. W. Norton, 1974.

Boehme, Franz M. *Altdeutsches Liederbuch*. Leipzig: Breitkopf and Haertel, 1877.

Bruce, D. D., Jr. *And They Sang Hallelujah*, Knoxville: University of Tennessee Press, 1974.

Brunk, George R. *Musical Instruments*. Carrollton, OH: Amish Mennonite Publications, n.d.

Burkhart, Charles. "The Church Music of the Old Order Amish." *Mennonite Quarterly Review* 27 (1953): 34.

———. "The Music of the Old Order Amish and the Old Colony Mennonites: A Contemporary Monodic Practice." MA thesis, Colorado College, 1952.

Christenpflicht. Scottdale, PA: Mennonite Publishing House, 1967.

Church and Sunday School Song Book. Scottdale, PA: Mennonite Publishing House, n.d.

Coblentz, John. *Music in a Biblical Perspective*. Harrisonburg, VA: Christian Light Publications, 1986.

Correll, Ernst. "The Value of Hymns for Mennonite History." *Mennonite Quarterly Review* 4 (July 1930): 215–19.

Durnbaugh, Hedwig T. "The Amish Singing Style: Theories of Its Origin and Description of Its Singularity." *Pennsylvania Mennonite Heritage* 22, no. 2 (1999): 24–31.

E., J. H. "Abner and His Cookies." *Family Life*, May 2001, 27–28.

Episcopal Church. *The Hymnal*. New York: Hymnal Corporation, 1940.

Erikson, Erik. *Childhood and Society*. New York: Norton, 1950.

Erk, Ludwig and Franz M. Böhme. *Deutscher Liederhort*. 3 vols. Leipzig: Breitkopf and Haertel, 1893. Repr. Hildesheim: Olms, 1963.

Fisher, Sara E. and Rachel K. Stahl. *The Amish School*. Intercourse, PA: Good Books, 1986.

Fishman, Andrea. *Amish Literacy: What and How It Means*. Portsmouth, NH: Heinemann, 1988.

———. *Language in Sociocultural Change*. Palo Alto, CA: Stanford University Press, 1972.

Foucault, Michel. *Madness and Civilization: A History of Insanity in the Age of Reason*. New York: Pantheon, 1965.

Frey, J. William. "Amish Hymns as Folk Music." In *Pennsylvania Songs and Legends*, edited by G. Korson. Philadelphia: University of Pennsylvania Press, 1949.

Gallagher, J. "Accepting Things Modern: An Interpretation of How the Amish Change." Paper presented at the International Conference on Coping with Modernity, Elizabethtown (PA) College, 1987.

Geertz, Clifford. *The Interpretation of Cultures: Selected Essays by Clifford Geertz*. New York: Basic Books, 1973.

———. "Religion as a Cultural System." In *Anthropological Approaches to the Study of Religion*, edited by Michael Banton. London: Tavistock, 2004.

Gerstner-Hirzel, Emily. *Das volkstümliche deutsche Wiegenlied: Versuch einer Typologie der Texte*. Basel: Schweizerischen Gesellschaft für Volkskunde, 1984.

Giroux, Henry A. *Border Crossings: Cultural Workers and the Politics of Education*. New York: Routledge, 1992.

Grauer, Victor. "Some Thoughts on Cross Cultural and Comparative Studies in Ethnomusicology." Unpublished paper, Mid-Atlantic Region, Society for Ethnomusciology, 2001.

Harms, Wolfgang. *Homo Viator in Bivio: Studien der Bildlichkeit des Weges*. Munich: Wilhelm Fink, 1970.

Harrell, Robert D. *Martin Luther, His Music, His Message*. Greenville, SC: Majesty Music, 1980.

Hausman, Ruth. *Sing and Dance with the Pennsylvania Dutch*. New York: Edward B. Marks, 1953.

Hohmann, Rupert Karl. "The Church Music of the Old Order Amish of the United States." PhD diss., Northwestern University, 1959.

Holy Bible, King James Version. King James Bible Online, 2008. www.kingjamesbibleonline.org.

Hostetler, John A. *Amish Society*. Baltimore: Johns Hopkins University Press, 1963.

———. *Educational Achievement and Lifestyles in a Traditional Society: The Old Order Amish*. Washington, DC: Office of Education Bureau of Research, Department of Health, Education, and Welfare, September 1969.

Hostetler, John A. and Gertrude Enders Huntington. *Amish Children: Education in the Family, School and Community*. 2nd ed. Fort Worth: Harcourt, Brace, Jovanovich, 1992.

———. *Children in Amish Society: Socialization and Community Education*. New York: Holt, Rinehart, Winston, 1971.

Huntington, Abbie Gertrude Enders. *Dove at the Window: A Study of the Old Order Amish*. Ann Arbor: University of Michigan Press, 1986.

———. "Persistence and Change in Amish Education." In The Amish Struggle with Modernity, edited by Donald B. Kraybill and Marc A. Olshan, 77–96. Elmira, Hanover, NH: University Press of New England, 1994.

Huntington, Gertrude Enders. "The Amish Family." In *Ethnic Families in America: Patterns and Variations*, edited by Charles H. Mindel and Robert W. Habenstein. 2nd ed. New York: Elsevier Scientific, 1981.

Hurst, Charles E. and David L. McConnell. *An Amish Paradox: Diversity and Change in the World's Largest Amish Community*. Baltimore: Johns Hopkins University Press, 2010.

Inspiring Favorites. Elmira, ON: Inspiring Favorites Publishers, 1992.

Jackson, George Pullen. "The American Amish Medieval Folk Tunes Today." *Southern Folklore Quarterly* 10 (1946): 151–57.

———. "The Strange Music of the Old Order Amish," *Musical Quarterly* 31, no. 3 (Jul 1945), 275–288.

Kauffman, Stanley. *Amish in Eastern Ohio*. Walnut Creek, OH: German Culture Museum, 1990.

Keeney, W. E. *The Development of Dutch Anabaptist Thought and Practice 1539–1564*. Nieukoop, Netherlands: B. de Graaf, 1968.

Keil, Charles. *Tiv Song*. Chicago: University of Chicago Press, 1979.

Keim, Albert. "From Erlanbach to New Glarus." In *Compulsory Education and the Amish: The Right Not to Be Modern*, edited by Albert Keim, 9–10. Boston: Beacon Press, 1975.

Klassen, Doreen. *Singing Mennonite: Low German Songs among the Mennonites*. Winnipeg: University of Manitoba Press, 1989.

Klees, Frederic. *The Pennsylvania Dutch*. New York: MacMillan, 1950.

Kingston, Joseph T. "The Amish Family." In *Ethnic Families in America: Patterns and Variations*, edited by Charles H. Mindel and Robert W. Habenstein. 2nd ed. New York: Elsevier Scientific Publishing, 1981.

———. "The Amish Story: Came to America Long Ago to Preserve Way of Life." *Intelligencer Journal* (Lancaster, PA), September 1953.

Klimuska, Ed. *Amish One-Room Schools: Lessons for the Plain Life*. Lancaster, PA: Lancaster Newspapers, n.d., n.p.

Kraybill, Donald. *Concise Encyclopedia of Amish, Mennonites, Hutterites*. Baltimore: Johns Hopkins University Press, 2010.

Kraybill, Donald B. and Carl F. Bowman. *On the Backroad to Heaven: Old Order Hutterites, Mennonites, Amish, and Brethren*. Baltimore: Johns Hopkins University Press, 2001.

Kraybill, Donald B., Karen M. Johnson-Weiner, and Steven M. Nolt. *The Amish*. Baltimore: Johns Hopkins University Press, 2013.

Kraybill, Donald B., Steven M. Nolt, and David L. Weaver-Zercher. *Amish Grace: How Forgiveness Transcended Tragedy*. San Francisco: Jossey-Bass, 2010.

Kraybill, Donald and Marc Olshan. *The Amish Struggle with Modernity*. Hanover, NH: University Press of New England, 1994.

Lapp, Mrs. Melvin, comp. *Heartland Hymns*. Neche, ND: Prairie View Press, 2005.

Levine, Lawrence W. *Black Culture and Black Consciousness*. New York: Oxford University Press, 1977.

Little, William and William Smith. *The Easy Instructor; or a New Method of Teaching Sacred Harmony*. Albany: Websters and Skinner and Daniel Steele, n.d. (1809).

Marglin, Stephen A. "Development as Poison: Rethinking the Western Model of Modernity." *Harvard International Review* 25, no. 1 (Spring 2003): 21–25.

Mast, John, ed. *The Duty of Children and Parents, Salvation Full and Free*. Hutchinson, KS: D & I Gospel Store, 1930.

McNamara, Patrick. "Introduction." In *Religion: North American Style*, edited by Thomas E. Dowdy and Patrick H. McNamara. 3rd ed. New Brunswick: Rutgers University Press, 1997.

Meyers, Thomas J. "The Amish Division: A Review of the Literature." In *Les Amish: Origine et particularismes, 1693*, edited by L. Hege and C. Wiebe, 40–53. Ingersheim, France: Association Française d'historier Anabaptiste-Mennonite, 1996.

Milicia, Joe. "*Amish Teens Rebel But Most Remain True to the Faith*." Worldwide Religious News, May 7, 2004. wwrn.org/articles/7298/?&section=amish.

Miller, Levi. *A Pilgrim's Search*. 1996, n.p.

Miller, Mary. *Our Heritage, Hope and Faith*. Walnut Creek, OH: Carlisle, 2000.

Nettl, Bruno. "The Hymns of the Amish: An Example of Marginal Survival." *Journal of American Folklore* 70, no. 278 (Oct–Dec 1957): 323–28.

———, ed. *The Study of Ethnomusciology: Twenty-Nine Issues and Concepts*. Urbana: University of Illinois Press, 1983.

Nolt, Steven M. *A History of the Amish*. Intercourse, PA: Good Books, 1992.

O'Day, Rosemary. *The Family and Family Relationships, 1500–1900: England, France and the United States of America*. New York: St. Martin's Press, 1994.

Ohio Amish Library. *Songs of the Ausbund: History and Translation of Ausbund Hymns*. Vol. 1, rev. Walnut Creek, OH: Carlisle Printing, 1998.

Overholt, John J., comp. *Erweckungs Lieder 1*. Sarasota, FL: Christian Hymnary Publishers, 1986.

Oyer, John S. "Is There an Amish Theology? Some Reflections on Amish Religious Thought and Practice." In *Les Amish: Origine et particularismes, 1693–1993*, edited by L. Hege and C. Wiebe, 278–302, Ingersheim, France: Association Française d'Histoire Anabaptiste-Mennonite, 1996.

Pamuk, Orhan. *Istanbul: Memories of a City*. London: Faber and Faber, 2005.

Piaget, Jean. *The Origins of Intelligence in Children*. New York: Oxford University Press, 1952.

"Problem Corner, The." *Family Life*, November 2006, 31–32.

Raber, John Paul. *Music—Harmonizing with the Truth*. Baltic, OH: Amish Brotherhood, n.d.

Ressler, Martin. "*Ein Unpartyeissche Liedersammlung's* 175th Anniversary." *Pennsylvania Mennonite Heritage* 2 (Oct 1979): 4.

Riall, R. A., trans., and G. A. Peters. *The Earliest Hymns of the Ausbund: Some Beautiful Christian Songs Composed and Sung in the Prison at Passau, Published in 1564.* Kitchener, ON: Pandora Press, 2003.

Ripa, Cesare. *Allegorie Dell'Iconologia di C. Ripa.* Rome: Cesare Ripa, 1603.

Rokicky, Catherine M. *Creating a Perfect World: Religious and Secular Utopias in Nineteenth-Century Ohio.* Athens: Ohio University Press, 2005.

Rose, Nikolas. *Governing the Soul: A Dialogue Account of Human Nature.* London: Routledge, 1990.

Sackville-West, V. *Nursery Rhymes.* London: Michael Joseph, 1950.

Schöne ausserlesene Figuren. Cited in *Homo Viator in Bivio: Studien der Bildlichkeit des Weges,* by Wolfgang Harms. Munich: Wilhelm Fink, 1970.

Smith, C. Henry. *The Mennonite Immigration to Pennsylvania in the Eighteenth Century.* Norristown, PA: Norristown Press, 1929.

Smucker, Melvin R. "How Amish Children View Themselves and Their Families: The Effectiveness of Amish Socialization." *Brethren Life and Thought* (Summer 1988), 218–236.

Sommers, Christiana Hoff. "Teaching the Virtues." *National Times,* June 1993, 3–13.

Songs of the Ausbund: History and Translation of Ausbund Hymns. Vol. 1, rev. Walnut Creek, OH: Carlisle Printing, 2001.

Nelson P. Springer. "The Editions of the Ausbund." In *Four Hundred Years with the Ausbund,* by Paul M. Yoder, E. Bender, H. Graber, and N. P. Springer, 31–40. Scottdale, PA: Herald Press, 1964.

Steel, David W. "Shape Note Singing Schools." In *Encyclopedia of Southern Culture,* edited by William Ferris and Charles Reagan Wilson. Chapel Hill: University of North Carolina Press, 1989. http://arts.state.ms.us/crossroads/music/sacred_harp/mu4_text.html.

Stokes, Martin, ed. *Ethnicity, Identity and Music: The Musical Construction of Place.* Oxford: Berg, 1994.

Stoll, Joseph, ed. *In meiner Jugend: A Devotional Reader in German and English.* Aylmer, ON: Pathway Publishers, 2000.

"Stranger and His Music, The." *Family Life,* December 2000, 14–16.

"Summary," *Blackboard Bulletin,* December 2006, 30.

Teacher Arlene [pseud.]. "The Singing Situation at Shady Lane School." *Blackboard Bulletin,* December 2000, 1–4.

Titon, Jeff Todd. *Worlds of Music.* New York: Schirmer, 1996.

Troyer, Ben, Jr. *Ausbund and Lieder Sammlung. Songs with Shape Notes.* Sugarcreek, OH: Carlisle Press, 1997.

Troyer, Ben, Jr., Jonathan Miller, and Mahlon Gingerich. *Ausbund and Lieder Sammlung Songs.* 2001.

Umble, John. "The Old Order Amish, Their Hymns and Hymn Tunes." *Journal of American Folklore* 52, no. 203 (Jan–Mar 1939): 82–95.

Unparteiische Liedersammlung, Eine. Aylmer, ON: Pathway Publishers, 1999. Originally published Elkhart, IN: Mennonitische Verlagsanstalt, 1892.

Unparteyishches Gesang-Buch, Eine. Lancaster, PA: George and Peter Albrecht, 1808.

Unparthenisches Gesang-Buch: Translations and Lessons. East Earl, PA: Schoolaid, 1997.

White, B. F., and E. J. King. *The Sacred Harp.* Philadelphia: T. K. and P. G. Collins, 1844.

Wittmer, Joe, and Arnold Moser. "Counseling the Old Order Amish Child." *Elementary School Guidance and Counseling* 8, no. 4 (May 1974): 263–71.

Wolf, J. Q., Jr. "The Death of Floyd Collins." 2002. www.lyon.edu/wolfcollection/songs /gingerdeath1266.html.

Wolkan, Rudolf. *Die Lieder der Wiedertäufer, Ein Beitrag zur deutschen und niederländischen Literatur- und Kirchengeschichte.* Berlin: Verlag B. Behr, 1903. Repr. Nieuwkoop, Netherlands: B. de Graff, 1965.

Yoder, Joseph W. *Amische Lieder.* Huntington, PA: Yoder Publishing, 1942.

Yoder, Paton and Steven R. Estes, eds. *Proceedings of the Amish Ministers' Meetings, 1862– 1878: Translation, Interpretation, Related Documents, Participants.* Goshen, IN: Mennonite Historical Society, 1999.

Yoder, Paul M., E. Bender, H. Graber, and N. P. Springer. *Four Hundred Years with the Ausbund.* Scottdale, PA: Herald Press, 1964.

Zahn, Johannes. *Die Melodien der deutschen evangelischen Kirchenlieder.* 6 vols. Guetersloh, Germany: Bertelemann, 1889–93.

Index

Werner O. Packull,
Hutterite Beginnings: Communitarian Experiments during the Reformation
Benjamin W. Redekop and Calvin W. Redekop, eds.,
Power, Authority, and the Anabaptist Tradition
Calvin Redekop, Stephen C. Ainlay, and Robert Siemens,
Mennonite Entrepreneurs
Calvin Redekop, ed., *Creation and the Environment:*
An Anabaptist Perspective on a Sustainable World
Steven D. Reschly, *The Amish on the Iowa Prairie, 1840 to 1910*
Kimberly D. Schmidt, Diane Zimmerman Umble, and Steven D. Reschly,
Strangers at Home: Amish and Mennonite Women in History
Diane Zimmerman Umble,
Holding the Line: The Telephone in Old Order Mennonite and Amish Life
David Weaver-Zercher, *The Amish in the American Imagination*